Romancing the Room

Romancing the Room

How to Engage Your Audience, Court Your Crowd, and Speak Successfully in Public

JAMES M. WAGSTAFFE
with **BRUCE BEAN**

THREE RIVERS PRESS
NEW YORK

Published by Three Rivers Press, New York, New York.
Member of the Crown Publishing Group, a division of Random House, Inc.

www.randomhouse.com

THREE RIVERS PRESS and the Tugboat design are registered trademarks
of Random House, Inc.

Printed in the United States of America

DESIGN BY ELINA D. NUDELMAN

Library of Congress Cataloging-in-Publication Data
Wagstaffe, James.
    Romancing the room : how to engage your audience, court your crowd, and
speak successfully in public / James Wagstaffe.–1st ed.
        p. cm.
    1. Public speaking.   I. Title.
PN4129.15.W34 2002
808.5'1–dc21   2001045694

ISBN 0-609-80597-5

10 9 8 7 6 5 4 3 2

First Edition

To Karen and PJ
for making us stop the talking and start the writing.

Acknowledgments

We were driving with our wives from San Francisco to Bakersfield one fall evening on a trip to a business conference. Crossing from Highway 101 to Interstate 5 we missed our usual turnoff and ended up driving through Priest Valley just south of Salinas. Talk turned to this book and the nagging topic of what its title should be. Thinking of the ever-present concept of "audience," Karen, Jim's wife, suggested *Romancing the Rows*. Interesting, but not quite right. And then it occurred to PJ, Bruce's wife: "How about *Romancing the Room*?" The metaphor was cast.

In countless ways this book has been an affair of the heart joined in by so many people, from our wives and children with their loving support to the many students who took risks to stand before an audience in over twenty years of speech classes at Stanford University. Each in his or her way has added to this text and brought life to these words. While it is impossible to acknowledge all the contributors, some stand out for their extra measures of devotion.

Thanks to Karen Wagstaffe for her good judgment in helping to select the most engaging stories; to PJ Bean for her good work as our literary flight controller; to our kids,

Michael, Emily, Matthew, and Megan Wagstaffe, and Maren and Trafton Bean, for being not the object of our stories but their subject; to Carrie Thornton for her marvelous editing that taught us our ABCs—apt, brief, and coherent; to Bonnie Solow for her gentle guidance and firm work as the most skilled literary agent one could hope to have; to Anne Pasley for enthusiastically teaching and orchestrating the speech class these past few years; to Jim Harville and Jai Marino for inspiring a love of speechmaking so many years ago; and to Ryan Dawson for enduring the task of transcribing Jim's spoken words to text.

Contents

Preface

It was the biggest day of the biggest trial of my career—in a case that had already reached the U.S. Supreme Court. Provocateur Jeffrey Masson was seeking millions of dollars from my client, the *New Yorker* magazine, based on alleged misquotations in a story written by famed writer Janet Malcolm. I was aggressively cross-examining Masson, while reporters from the *New York Times* to *Vanity Fair* made their records for posterity. All eyes in the courtroom were transfixed on this legal pas de deux. The pace was so fast and intense that one newspaper later reported that "every time Wagstaffe spoke, the court reporter closed her eyes, tilted her head back and transformed into a blind jazz pianist!"

Not everyone wants to be a trial attorney. However, doesn't capturing an audience's attention sound appealing to you? Wouldn't you rather have others think of you as interesting and influential, rather than boring and uninspired? Do you worry that when you stand up to speak, others not only look at their watches, but also shake them to see if they're still working?

The challenge of any good communicator is to connect

with your listeners, to make your points—to "romance the room." Communicating with others in a group setting has all the elements of a good romance: getting over the jitters and making a good first impression, putting your best side forward, making it clear where things are going, and keeping things interesting by spicing up the relationship. Simply put, you must engage your audience and court your crowd—romance them—if you want to speak successfully in public.

There are many rooms in which you must romance and woo your audience: engaging students in the classroom, targeting business clients in the boardroom, or reeling in your off-to-the-mall teenager in the family room. Being a trial lawyer and having taught Practical Speech Communication at Stanford for over twenty years, I make my living with my mouth (see www.wagstaffe.com). But effective communication is essential to all our lives—whether we know it or not.

If you live to talk and you come from a family of talkers as I do, there is always a ready-made audience at the constant family gatherings. From as early as I can remember, my mom and dad presided over "family table talks" where one was expected to opine about some topic chosen from the day's current event to the value of some designated object in the room.

I remember one such table talk like it was yesterday. It was a weeknight around the dinner table when my dad handed me a pretzel with this instruction: "Stand and talk." I held the pretzel, addressed the gathered masses (my parents and two of my siblings), and described the source of the pretzel in question: our local downtown pretzel stand. After every purchase of one of the delicacies, the vendor would beam with pride, saying he made the "very best pretzel in America!" I said that this was what made our country great—the fact that a pretzel maker from a little California town could still strive for excellence . . . to make the very best pretzel.

I do the same thing today—no doubt to the great chagrin of each of my four children. Recently, I, too, presided over an evening's table talk exercise, handed *my* teenage son Michael an eraser, and commanded: "Stand and talk." Unfazed (although perhaps annoyed), Michael said that we'd all like to have "redos" in our lives, to erase those events or choices that in hindsight we've come to regret. However, this is not right, Michael remarked. It is from the past, good and bad, that we learn the lessons of our lives. An eraser could also erase the lessons. He said, "We should not erase the past pictures of our lives, but rather color them in!"

Listening to Michael speak, I realized that it isn't easy having a communications teacher for a father, but boy, was I proud.

After both my parents passed away within a few months of each other several years ago, I came to understand that there were simple but profound lessons in these table topic presentations. There is such value in learning to communicate, to engage and move listeners. I promised myself that like the pretzel maker, it was time for me to strive to be the best. I would try to share my thoughts and experiences on communicating to a wide variety of listeners. That is why I wrote this book—to share the romance of effective communication.

PART 1

Romancing the Room Principles

CHAPTER 1

Falling in Love

Most of us have only one or two true romances in our lives. These are times when we have a heightened awareness of how one other person perceives us, and what we can do to make the desired favorable impression on him or her. During this time we are acutely aware that the way we communicate with this object of our affection, and the words we use, control the way we are viewed.

On many levels, we all become experts on the communication of romance without even knowing it. Most of you will agree with the following romance truisms:

- **Personalize your charm.** It's not just in the movies that the guy gets the girl because he's done his homework about her wants and desires. A romance will work if each person is aware of the other's background and experiences. Is it any surprise that most dates (and job interviews, for that matter) are viewed most favorably if you talk almost exclusively about the other person?

- **Avoid turnoffs and find common ground.** The key to successful romances often depends on finding common activities and interests. Acting or speaking in ways that are turnoffs can kill a budding romance. For every

Mary Matalin–James Carville "political opposites" marriage, there are hundreds of failed romances because "we don't have anything in common."

- **Maintain the romance.** Sustaining a romance is the real challenge. How does one maintain the mutual love interest without the relationship becoming stale? Marriage counselors tell us that one must vary routines and add variety to keep the spice in a romantic relationship.

These are truisms for romance because they are truisms for all successful interpersonal communications. You must get someone's immediate attention, control it favorably, and then sustain it over a longer period of time. These interactive principles remain true whether the communication is a speech to a local service club, a toast at a family gathering, or a closing argument to a jury. You must get and then keep your audience.

This is not a book on romance per se. Rather, it is about a technique of communicating with others, whether in large groups or one-on-one, in a way that engages the listeners' attention. In many ways, you get the listeners to "fall in love" with you and your message. A successful speaker or communicator "romances the room" in order to achieve the desired purpose.

Our Attention Deficit Culture

You can't romance any room if the listeners aren't paying attention. As we will see, this obstacle is not always so easy to overcome.

In today's world of e-mail, facsimiles, and voice messages, the number of communications we encounter is escalating at an ever-increasing rate. For example, it's been estimated that the average American is exposed to over three thousand commercial messages daily. There are over a million meetings and approximately 33 million presentations occurring every day in this country alone—to say nothing about the hundreds of millions of interpersonal communications taking place throughout the land.

It is no surprise, therefore, that the average person's attention span has dwindled rapidly in the face of such an avalanche of messages. As we will see later, ours is an attention deficit culture. One need only think of the television viewer clutching the remote while channel surfing or the computer aficionado surfing the web to understand the instant synapse-to-neuron nature of today's world.

In today's attention deficit culture, it is imperative for communicators to be instantly memorable, empowering, and authentic. Perhaps the greatest challenge for any communicator is to overcome the increasingly limited attention spans of modern listeners and engage them with more extended communications.

There's no question that we have many modern communication tools at our disposal, including computer-generated graphics, videotaped rehearsal sessions, meetings by teleconference, instant e-mail messages, and focus group preparation. However, with all this updated gadgetry and sophistication, are we communicating any more effectively or to our maximum potential? Are we communicating with any more understanding and compassion for the listener? Have the rapid-fire exchanges of chat rooms replaced the shared imaginings of the campfire story? Is a teleconference really the same as being there in person? Have we lost the ability to romance a room?

These are the questions facing every communicator coming of age in the twenty-first century. No matter what the setting or the number of modern tools, effective communication still comes down to creating a relationship between the speaker and the listener. Speakers still must use words, images, and stories to captivate the attention of any listener or audience. It is in understanding the romance quality of communications that we can overcome the obstacles of our modern age and achieve our communication goals.

The Techniques for Romancing the Room

The thesis of this book is that the techniques of personal romance can be adapted directly to all public speaking settings. Communication begins like a blind date: without anxiety, one secures a *favorable first impression* and then *aims to win approval*. You must notice and address your listeners' "wandering eye"—with the realization that your audience's attention is a precious commodity that should not be squandered through unclear communication objectives, verbal digressions, or nonverbal distractions.

Just as in a personal romance, great communicators build *relationships* with their listeners. By asking questions about the audience in advance, speakers can maximize the effectiveness of their message. Communicators must listen while they talk, adapting to the audience's response, be it restlessness, confusion, or disagreement.

Distractions and boredom often are the great turnoffs to any relationship. Great communicators who want to romance a room must avoid flat or repetitive voice patterns, distracting body language, and personal idiosyncrasies. But it is more than delivery that makes for engaging communication. We also must to learn how better to use sweet talk (i.e., vivid language and compelling images) to romance any listener. There is also great benefit to bringing flowers and candy (using communication tools) to win over any person or group.

The techniques of *Romancing the Room* can be applied to

a variety of communication types. For example, "The Sales Room" shows how to win a customer's (or anyone else's) love for you and your idea. "The Family Room" reveals the secrets for connecting with our spouses and children (including our teenagers!). "The Ballroom" describes techniques for entertaining others and being the life of the party or the podium. "The Classroom" will let all readers (and teachers) learn how to make learning lovable and unforgettable. "The Money Room" discusses fund-raising skills and how one can painlessly ask individuals or groups for financial contributions.

One can romance these and other audiences in captivating style. Years ago, the goal was to "Win Friends and Influence People." These skills of engagement are even more important today. Whether their goal is to seal the big deal, get the perfect job, or inspire their teenager to score winning grades, effective communicators aim to get their listeners to say yes to their points for the long term. Just as in romance, tedium and disinterest are the enemies. Thus, the one room communicators must never enter is the bored room.

A Little Personal Romance

Next time you are in the presence of family members or a couple turning the pages of a photo album, look at their eyes. They glisten with the joy of the remembered experience. Married couples can often rekindle their romance by remembering to remember their prior shared joys.

Speakers seeking to romance a room will increase their effectiveness by speaking about or creating shared experiences with the audience. Reference to common experiences builds a powerful and lasting bond between speaker and audience.

Personalizing a presentation is the ticket to success. We will later explore the value of making common references to the audience's background and experiences. If the speech occurs on a special day for the group or community (e.g., the founder's birthday), a reference to that matter connects the speaker to the audience. Whether the speaker is trying to persuade, inform, or entertain the group, this personal touch will help win the day, and avoid later disconnects.

The personal approach to romancing the room also includes the speaker sharing stories with the audience. Storytelling, also the subject of a later chapter, is an essential part of effective exposition. When you share stories about yourself or others, the audience connects with you, and remembers the presentation. Ask yourself what you remember about the most recent speech or presentation you heard. Wasn't it the story or stories that were told (e.g., "that guy who talked about his family's wild trip to Yosemite")?

There's a reason why great comedians, teachers, and after-dinner speakers make use of their own lives and families to make their points. These stories not only spring from the well of their own experiences (and thus are more authentic), they unite speaker with audience in a way that no words or images otherwise can.

Bear with me as I share stories, personal and otherwise, throughout this book. They will give both context and meaning as we explore the subject of romancing the room—and hopefully entertain you as well!

There's nothing like a good story to start and eventually seal the romance. I try to keep track of the audiences with whom I've shared certain stories or anecdotes. However, someone recently told me that I shouldn't worry so much about the folly of repeating a good story to people who have heard it before, because they will enjoy it listening to it again. As many times as I've seen the movie *Casablanca,* I still love it when I'm channel surfing on a Saturday afternoon and this classic is on TV. And when they sing "The Marseillaise" at Rick's Cafe, I puddle up every time.

A good many of us have that ultimate story of romantic connection: how we first met the person with whom we are sharing our lives.

For me, it was the first day of my third year of law school. I walked (some might say trolled) through the library and saw an attractive young woman reading her casebook at one of the study tables. Noticing that she was reading a famous civil procedure case, *Pennoyer v. Neff,* I sat down and struck up a conversation. We got to talking about civil procedure (my then and still favorite legal subject) and what was then her first day of her first year of law school. One thing led to another—a follow-up date, a series of shared experiences, and almost exactly three years later, a wedding to my wife, Karen.

CHAPTER 2

The Blind Date Challenge

We've all heard of "love at first sight," but most would-be romances are made or broken in the first few moments. I'll bet if you took a poll of the two participants in the first thirty seconds of a blind date, and then again at the end of the night, the favorability ratings wouldn't change much with increased exposure.

First impressions in communication are like first impressions on a blind date: not only do they matter, they are crucial. A bad first impression is hard to overcome. It has been estimated that if someone makes a bad first impression, it takes as many as nine future interactions to overcome the initial negative reaction.

A Psych I study proves it. The first group of test subjects are shown a picture of a cat and asked to say what it is. Slowly, over the course of many pictures, the image is morphed into that of a dog. The test subjects who started out with the image of a cat are much slower to change their answer to a dog than the second group of subjects, who come in midstream and see a picture of a dog at the outset. As a listener or viewer you remain loyal to your first impression.

One wants to control negative first impressions if possible. I remember an attorney applicant who came through our office some time ago for a series of interviews. I was the third partner in the office to meet with him. When the young man walked into my office I noticed immediately that one of his button-down collars was just the opposite–unbuttoned and standing at an upward, full-staff salute. I formed a first impression (negative, if not pitying) from that first image. But I also wonder to this day how two of the partners could have made it through their interviews without telling this poor fellow about his wardrobe predicament!

An even more common example of the first impressions principle takes place when a professor walks into a classroom on the first day of the course. Whether the teacher is late or prompt, whether his or her appearance is rumpled or crisp, and his or her first few words all contribute mightily to students' first impressions of the upcoming semester's experience. In fact, studies show that students have remarkably fixed views even at that early stage.

As a trial lawyer, I am acutely aware of the significance of first impressions. Almost all the studies reveal that a jury's mind is virtually made up at the end of the opening statements. If you don't hook the jury at the outset, you'll lose it.

All good communicators spend a great deal of time planning their openers and examining themselves so as to avoid creating negative first impressions. This involves clothing, appearance, presentation, and content. I take a Polaroid snapshot of myself on certain occasions (before an interview, before speaking to a big audience, before making a closing argument) to see what it is like to look at me. I also market test my introduction (meaning I try it out first on my wife). I stop after just one minute to get her first impression. It's not surprising that politicians and comedians test their openers to see what works.

I always tell my children to get an A on the first exam of a semester. Not only does this make a favorable first impression on the teacher, it also creates what I call "positive academic momentum." The teacher thinks you're an A student and therefore views your future papers and assignments through that prism. It's harder to change from that positive first impression to one that is negative. It goes without saying that the opposite is even more true.

Therefore, it is essential to have never-fail openers for *any* communication. The positive momentum principle applies to small and large group communications as well as to academia. Try any one of the following beginnings:

1. **The Grabber.** This is where the first words spoken "grab" the audience, snatching its attention at the outset. For example, a student in my speech class at Stanford some years ago started her speech by saying, "I'm a cox." After we recovered from the shock of the sound of this not so common appellation, she went on to tell us about the unique skills needed by the coxswain of a boat for a crew team. I knew of a criminal defense lawyer who employed the Grabber technique at the beginning of his summation to the jury. He started by handing out airsickness bags to each member of the jury. He announced, "I know you'll need these after what you have just heard from the prosecution!" The jury certainly wanted to know what came next.

2. **The Curiosity Arousal.** Great communicators often start their presentations or communications with an idea or image that piques the curiosity of the listeners. If your curiosity is aroused, you'll pay attention because you want to know what happens next. For example, a student in my class started off her speech the following way: "Lines. There are lines all around us. As the wall meets the ceiling, that forms a line. As the door meets its

edge, that forms a line. And there are lines in your hand." The speaker then went on with a fascinating description of the meaning of lines in the hand and how one reads palms.

3. **The Problem to Solve.** One never-fail introduction presents a problem for the audience and the speaker to work through together. The communicator sets the stage with a question to be answered or a problem to be solved. One must, of course, convince the audience that it is a problem worth solving. For example, a student in my class one year opened his visual aid speech by posing this challenge: "Would you like to see me drink a flaming tequila without burning my mustache?" Now, this was a problem we wanted to see him solve . . . and he did. He taught us throughout the course of his speech how to avoid the burning issue raised at the outset of his speech!

4. **The Hey, Yeah.** It is beneficial to begin a presentation with a Hey, Yeah statement. This means saying something that immediately engages the audience and causes it to agree with or acknowledge the intrinsic reality of a statement. For example, comedians often utilize the Hey, Yeah method for sustaining attention. They make references to everyday occurrences to which we can relate. I gave a speech once on the value of slowing down on the highways and commented on the then-recent law that had reduced speed limits to fifty-five miles per hour. I said that we had lost speed, but we had gained a sense of calm and wonder. As it turned out, this was a common reaction of my listeners, and they were able to say, "Hey, yeah, that's true."

5. **The "Whoa" Introduction.** While the grabber says something that gets your immediate attention, the Whoa introduction causes the listener to be taken off guard and stunned at the outset. A speech that I gave many years ago began with a series of words spoken very rapidly: "Lunar modules, tranquilizers, sticky tape, the Beatles, quadraphonic sound, tape recorders, instant food, wash and wear, jet planes." I then said, "Oh, am I speaking too fast? I only have ten minutes, you know." The idea was to catch the au-

dience off guard as well as to audibly illustrate the point of my speech, which was about the rapid rate of change in our society.

6. **Presuming Audience Involvement.** Most speeches start by introducing one's self to the audience and introducing the persons or ideas that will populate the topic. However, sometimes speeches start in the middle because the communicator presumes (without explanation) that the audience is already involved. For example, one of my students started the first speech of the spring semester as follows; "I didn't know what I was going to say to Brad over spring break." She then went on to tell us that her best friend in high school had become paralyzed in a skiing accident and that she was planning to visit him during spring break. Notice that she doesn't say, "I have a friend; his name is Brad; he was a friend of mine in high school." Rather, she starts the speech as if we already know about Brad and their friendship.

7. **The Room Reference.** It rarely fails to begin a communication with a reference to something that is familiar to the listeners. In an interview, one can comment upon photographs or icons that the interviewer has chosen to place in her or his office. Similarly, our reference to a certain occasion or to the special interest of the listeners will work. This also might include a reference to what a preceeding speaker has said.

8. **The Movie Preview.** We watch movie previews because they whet our appetites for what is to come. A good "never-fail" introduction does the same thing. We want to see more of the movie because we have been given enough details that we are interested in how it turns out. This introduction gives listeners a preview of the coming attractions. (Of course, this kind of introduction begs for the review at the end of the speech to confirm that we got our money's worth . . . and a little popcorn to boot.)

So good communication is like a blind date; it's important to make a favorable first impression. However, anyone who's ever been on such an escapade knows that even if the first few seconds and minutes go well you can't just coast along . . . otherwise there will be no second date. So, as you begin your speech and think of how to get the audience's attention, you must be planning a second date. This will include, as we will see below, techniques for sustaining attention and maintaining variety throughout the presentation. The best way to avoid the wandering eye syndrome is to know exactly who is listening to you and what it is that will motivate them to continue paying attention.

CHAPTER 3

The Wandering Eye Syndrome

There may be no greater challenge to a communicator attempting to romance listeners than the "wandering eye syndrome." Your listeners seem distracted, maybe even bored with what you are saying. Like in a failing romance, the bloom is off the rose when listeners daydream and their attention strays.

It can happen in any communication and at almost any time. Maybe it's the voice mail that goes on too long, or the phone call you are dying to interrupt with an "It's been nice talking to you." There isn't a teenager alive who hasn't rolled his or her eyes in the face of what he or she perceives as another long lecture. We have all endured interviews, wishing they weren't twenty-minute sessions. The wandering eye syndrome is a common affliction among meeting participants and people sitting through after-dinner speeches.

There have been volumes written on how to read someone's body language, and how to spot a wandering eye. But there are obvious signs of distraction in the unromanced room, and I want to help you to be able to spot them quickly.

- Wandering eyes
- Shifting bodies in chairs
- Yawns
- Not so subtle glances at the watch
- Glances at the clock on the wall
- Slowing pace of note taking
- An absence of responses to interactive techniques

As mentioned previously in chapter 1, we live in an attention deficit world. It has been estimated that the average attention span of an adult is seven minutes. How amazingly common it is to see computer users tapping their fingers impatiently if the modem takes more than ten seconds to connect.

It is probably no accident that the average seven-minute attention span of adults equals the typical interval between commercials on television programs. With the present generation reared on twenty thousand hours of television by the age of eighteen, speakers have to be more engaging than the catchiest product commercials.

Those with whom we speak have come to expect synthesized communications, or what one of my friends calls the *USA Today* version of events. Sometimes it seems that we are fed nothing but sound bites. How long do you think the average story on the TV nightly news is? Twenty-three words. No wonder we've been called the channel-surfing generation. We can easily switch from station to station, capturing just enough information or content to keep us apprised.

But most of life's communications are *more* than twenty-three words. When you're teaching a class, addressing a congregation, or making a sales pitch, you need to expand the audience's attention span. You need to make them lose track of time, and avoid the wandering eye syndrome.

We have all faced the wandering eye syndrome as listeners' attentions vary. Even effective communicators know the following attention span reality: one-third of your listeners are listening with rapt attention; another third are like an old radio, tuning you in and tuning you out; and the final third are somewhere else completely–planning the lineup for their baseball team's, writing a grocery list, or maybe indulging in sexual fantasies!

In any event, they are not attentive to your message. This slightly exaggerated description illustrates that it is difficult to keep a listener paying full attention to a communication for an extended period of time. There is a great temptation to throw up one's arms and simply accept that people today have lost the ability to listen with any degree of attentiveness. After all, we communicate like hummingbirds, making only instant contact with each recipient. Don't write a letter; send an e-mail. Why make personal contact? Leave a voice mail. Time to reflect? No way. Respond by fax and FedEx. Read the whole article? Nothing doing. Just get the summary and surf the Web.

The problem is not simply that we speed through our lives, but that we also are hyperaware of time itself. We calculate how long every activity in our schedule will take ... to the minute. The airplane not only travels from Los Angeles to New York faster, but in exactly 4 hours and 58 minutes. Microwave ovens furnish our holiday turkeys in precisely 47 minutes, and Minute Rice makes it onto your table in just 60 seconds.

And you know, an interesting thing has happened. As technology increases the rapidity with which we can do things, psychologically we feel that merely because we *can* do it faster, we *should* do it faster. Thus, the exact length of each of our activities, and the speed with which we are compelled to complete them, leads us to time slot our lives, with seemingly little time to pay attention to extended discourse. The irony, of course, is that the more technology provides us with tools to expedite our lives, the more we cry, "I just don't have enough time."

Our way of adapting is to "PowerBar" our communications, packing as much as possible into as small amount of time as possible . . . before we go on to the next communication. We read *USA Today* because the articles end in five paragraphs. Readership studies show that people peruse the headlines and very little else. In fact, there's an entire network devoted to "headline news."

We expect our information instantly, and our attention span requires diversity of information. The free-and-easy image of surfing from the early 1960s has resurfaced today in an entirely different context. We channel surf and surf the Web, and if a site doesn't grab us immediately, then it's on to the next one.

When you do communicate with others, you are in constant conflict with competing communicators in the media. It's been estimated that a typical person is exposed to over three thousand commercial messages each day. It seems inconceivable that we could follow the seventeen thousand new grocery-store products that were introduced last year . . . but the next time you walk through the supermarket, count the thousands of products you could (and subliminally will) notice.

These commercial messages are everywhere. Forget the ads on the seventy cable channels at home; they've now got televisions in the airport, advertisements in elevators, and product endorsements in public rest rooms. Check out the attire on professional athletes, or on the sides, tops, and maybe bottoms of stock cars—there's a product endorsement on every square inch of available space. You simply cannot get from website to website without confronting an avalanche of commercial messages—starting from the moment you go for your e-mail (and must click to say "no thank you" to the day's featured product) to the tedious task of deleting that day's spam. They even get you when you're not looking, filling our movies and magazines with well-researched and expensive product placements for goods as varied as M&M's, tickets, and Gatorade!

And all this is happening as Americans are feverishly clocking 60-hour weeks to do the mountain of work that needs to be done. Americans have the unfortunate distinction of being the world's leaders in the number of hours worked each year (1,966 hours), surpassing even the Japanese by about 70 hours. On average, Americans work 350 hours more per year (that's almost nine full workweeks) than Europeans.

None of this, however, means that we should give up in our quest to engage or arouse others with words and images. Rather, the challenge is simply greater. People still can get engrossed in a good book or a hit movie . . . oblivious to the passage of time. A great stage actor or storyteller can mesmerize an audience such that time flies by.

Do you remember being so engrossed by a communication that time seemed to be suspended? Perhaps it was on a first date when suddenly, after hours of enthralling conversation, you realized the restaurant workers were putting the chairs up on the tables, preparing to close for the night. Maybe it was a long car trip where an engaging book on tape turned miles into what seemed to be the blink of an eye. On occasion, a three-hour movie goes by in what seems to be just minutes. We all, at one time or another, experience communications that are so absorbing that time passes without notice.

When I was in my last year of law school, I took my wife to see Richard Burton play King Arthur in his last run of the play *Camelot.* A struggling law student, I bought the cheap seats in the rafters of the cavernous Golden Gate Theater in San Francisco. With a thousand people eyeing him at the edge of the footlights, Burton delivered the marvelous soliloquy at the end of the first act, pondering the conflict in his status as a man who loved his wife and his best friend, and his role as the king who must punish Queen Guinevere's and Lancelot's treasonous affair. As the curtain fell, not a sound could be heard. There was a transfixed silence, followed by thunderous applause. There wasn't a wandering eye in the house.

CHAPTER 4

The Communicator's Courtship

No romance will ever work unless there is a dedicated courtship process. Courting someone else includes presenting yourself in an engaging manner, while you learn more and more about the other person.

For communicators, the courtship begins with making a good first impression on the "blind date." However, you continue the courtship (and maintain the listeners' attention) by learning about and appealing to the audience's values and interests. People understandably tend to fall in love with those who are interested in them. Company presidents hire workers who listen to their needs and seem interested. Teenagers understand a reference to MTV more immediately than they would to National Public Radio. Simply put, effective speakers know the ABC of all communication: audience before content. Know who you are speaking to and then adapt your content and supporting materials to that audience.

Keeping Your "Eye off the I"

In order to understand your listeners, you must learn their backgrounds, know the communication situation, observe body language, and be ever ready to adapt. You can succeed in all of these areas by adopting the "eye off the I" principle. In all communication, whether public speaking or in small group settings, solipsism is dangerous. If you focus only on what is interesting to you, you'll end up with a romance that fizzles instead of sizzles.

The essential techniques for keeping your eye off the I are as follows:

- **Use first person plural** . . . literally and figuratively. When speaking with others, include them by referring to "our" issues or things "we" can do. Include the audience in your thought process and involve them in the issues you raise. Of course, you must start with issues that will be interesting and of value to them.

- **Use first names.** Salespersons have learned an important technique: use your customers' first names to bring them into your ideas. Make allusions to your listeners' common experiences and illustrate your points with examples that are consonant with their experience.

- **Speak for a shorter time than expected.** As addressed before, the communicator must be ever aware of the audience's attention span. Learn how long you are expected to speak, and then speak for a shorter period of time. Your audience will be pleased and will remember you.

- **Sit in the audience.** When you are speaking, imagine yourself sitting in the audience. Michael Jordan, the famous professional basketball player, used to say that one should "be the ball." Great communicators learn to "be the listener." For example, I have tried many a jury trial during which I have adapted this principle to "be the juror." I imagine what it is like to sit in a jury, to have waited all day before selection, and to be confronted by sometimes boring, sometimes nearly incomprehensible evidence. To wake the jury up, I try to shake it up, by presenting different images and by varying my pacing in questioning witnesses.

Target Your Message

As with target marketing, all good communications start with an understanding of the composition and the backgrounds of your listeners. Ask yourself the following questions:

- What is the attitude of the listeners toward you?
- What is the attitude of the listeners toward your subject?
- What is the attitude of the listeners toward the occasion?
- What is the general age of the group?
- What is the size of the audience?
- What is the educational background of the group?
- What is their occupation or field of work?
- What is their knowledge and background regarding the subject matter?
- Who has spoken to the group before?
- What is the gender makeup of the audience?
- What is their family status?
- What are their politics and memberships?
- What are their sources of information and entertainment?

I gain this information by observing the group before I communicate, by inquiring of those who normally run the meeting or ask me to speak, and by occasionally asking questions directly of the group at the beginning of the presentation. Whether the communication is a million-dollar jury trial or a fund-raising speech for a civic organization, you must learn what will work by asking who is there.

Imagine the failed demographic in the speech given in my Practical Speech Communication class at Stanford University several years ago. The speaker delivered a speech titled "How to Set Up the Pieces in a Game of Backgammon." Using an elaborate and enlarged metal backgammon board, the student attached magnetic pieces for demonstrative purposes. At the end of what was a rather simple presentation, the class seemed listless and disinterested. So I posed the question that was obviously not researched before the speech: "How many of you regularly play backgammon?" The answer was unanimous—the audience was already familiar with the basics of the game. The speech was pitched at far too low a level and proceeded to bore an otherwise highly involved audience.

This can happen to the best of us. Some years ago, I was speaking to a statewide commerce association advancing the thesis that commercial growth should be slowed because of the pressure on our natural resources and the challenges of solid waste disposal. In the question and answer session after my speech, a member of the association asked me my thoughts as to the feasibility of locating disposal plants (and ultimately entire cities) in space. Glibly, I responded that the idea was far-fetched and "more fanciful than RoboCop!" The audience went deathly silent. What I didn't know was that one month before, a Nobel laureate from the local university had addressed the group and made that very suggestion!

The Search for Shared Meaning

There is a reason why courtship doesn't work when the two participants don't speak the same language. They are unable to understand each other, and the physical attraction of the blind date cannot sustain the relationship.

The same is true for those who communicate with audiences in large or small settings. As a threshold requirement, speakers must use words and stories that are comprehensible to their listeners. References to common experiences (e.g., a hit movie, a bestseller, the top-of-the-fold news story) will enhance the speaker's courtship effort. One cannot accomplish any communication objective unless the speaker and the audience achieve a shared meaning.

At its most basic level (and as will be explored later in the "Classroom" chapter), the speaker must define any terms that are not known by the audience. This is particularly necessary in speeches on complicated or technical subjects. However, many speakers fall into technical jargon with little concern or awareness that the audience has long been lost on the topic. This no doubt is the reason that I am an attorney (not a doctor), insofar as my collegiate foray into organic chemistry stalled in the first week of class. I just didn't grasp the jargon.

A few years ago, I went shopping at the local drug store. For reasons that are too arcane for expression here, I was looking to buy a Ken doll (you know, Barbie's erstwhile companion). I asked the store clerk where I could make this purchase, and she immediately responded by directing me to Aisle 6. When I got there, I found no Ken doll, but I did find a whole row of *candles*.

Good speakers do not want such verbal ships to pass in the night. You want to ensure that what you are saying is what they are hearing. For example, as a teacher, I randomly ask one of my students to let me look over his or her notes—not because I want to pass judgment on the notes, but rather because I want to pass judgment on me. Am I using language, examples, and expressions that are clear? Are my students taking notes that accurately and fully capture the meaning of my class lectures? If not, I must define terms more clearly and reiterate points that might have been lost.

Sometimes the mixed signals on language can be more amusing. When I was growing up, whenever my parents had another couple over for dinner, the three younger kids (of whom I was one) were paraded out in our pajamas to greet the guests at the door before we were sent upstairs to bed. On one such occasion when I was eight years old, my older brother Steve (a mischievous twelve-year-old) suggested something for me to say to Mrs. White when she and Mr. White were greeted at the door that evening. Dutifully, I stood up tall (in my footed pajamas) and proclaimed to Mrs. White: "My, you look *promiscuous* tonight!" I was sent immediately to bed.

Listen While You Talk

As a speech teacher, a trial lawyer, and a lecturer, I am often asked for advice on how to *read* one's audience. I always respond with this phrase: *Listen while you talk.* What I mean by this is that effective communication requires an ongoing awareness not only of the listeners' backgrounds and interests, but also of their actual reactions during the speech itself. If you "listen" to your audience at this room level, your ultimate courtship of them will be successful.

If you want your listeners to fall in love with you and your ideas, you must be attentive to the way in which they are experiencing the presentation. In modern parlance, this is often referred to as the way the listeners are "processing" the content of the speech. Too many communicators fail to take the temperature of their listeners, and thus fail in their courtship effort.

For example, if an audience seems bored or restless, consider using more humor and novelty, using more concrete examples, making direct references to the audience, and inviting its participation. Ask the audience to give examples or to raise their hands to denote agreement. Illuminate technical presentations and numbers by focusing more on imagery and example. Make your delivery more animated. Change your location in the room by walking around the lectern or sitting on a desk. And most importantly, cut it short. Eliminate the subpoints, drive home your thesis sentence, and stop.

Bill Clinton is a master at "listening" to an audience, especially in his favorite setting, the town meeting. In that seemingly relaxed environment, the former president is able to avoid the stilted look of a debate or a formal speech, and interacts with the people. He has been said to "feel their pain" by listening carefully to their questions, using first names, and making references to local persons or events. Even if the localizing effort was the result of skilled advance persons and index cards, President Clinton, like many a skilled politician, has been able to project an image of genuine interest.

We often test the ongoing success of our own romantic courtships by speaking with our partner's friends or when we overhear their communications with others about the relationship. Test your courtship efforts. During a break in your presentation, be a fly on the wall and listen to what people are saying about you and your message. At the end, sneak a peak at someone's notes and see what they understood to be the thrust of your remarks.

I tried this in a recent speech of mine on the First Amendment cases heard in a concluded U.S. Supreme Court term. I was on the dais during a break, and I overheard a colleague on the faculty say to another professor: "His presentation really is quite *discursive.*" Unfortunately, this undercover effort was not of much help because I didn't know the meaning of the descriptive adjective. It wasn't until I got home that I learned it wasn't the highest of compliments!

Vary the Proofs

When a lawyer introduces evidence in a trial to make a point, it is referred to as proof. We learn that to keep a jury interested, we must vary the type of proof or we risk boring them or even putting them to sleep.

The concept of using supporting materials that require a varied response from an audience is widely used in public presentations. For example, a singer putting on a concert will not sing all fast songs or all softer tunes. Rather, he or she will vary the program in order to keep the audience involved.

When a speaker addresses an audience, the same varied proof principle applies. Speakers use various materials, or "proofs" (e.g. stories, facts, illustrations, quotations, etc.) to support their points. The ancient Greek orators, most notably Aristotle, broke these proofs into three categories.

1. **Logos.** We are most accustomed to the form of proof known as "logos"—or logical proof. We demonstrate our points by utilizing points of logic as proof. We make the point with supporting statistics and logical analysis. For example, if you were trying to persuade an audience of grandparents that they should always buckle their very young grandchildren into car seats, you would present logical statistics as to the number of deaths that result when the strict requirements of the law are not followed.

2. **Ethos.** A speaker can also ask an audience to accept a point made in a presentation by appealing to the form of proof known as "ethos"—or ethical proof. You should accept the speaker's position on a point because of their credibility on the matter (or the borrowed credibility obtained from source materials or quotations). So, to follow our example, you could prove your point about the car seat requirement by bringing in a highway patrol officer

who can share his or her views on the subject. The matter is proved because a person with credibility has supported it.

3. **Pathos.** Finally, speakers can prove their points by reliance on "pathos"—or emotional proof. Rather than utilizing logical or credibility-based proof, a communicator can appeal to the audience's emotions in order to support a point made in a speech. These emotions can be humor, drama, poignancy, and so on. To complete our example on the speech to the grandparents about car seats, imagine that the speaker says the following:

I was reading a recent letter to Dear Abby on this subject. It said: "Dear Abby: Please share my experience with your readers. It was a Saturday morning, and our beloved three-year-old boy was wrenching with what seemed to be a whooping cough. My husband and I needed to drive him to the doctor's office right away. My boy was coughing so spasmodically that I decided to put him on my lap in the front seat for the short half-mile drive to the medical center. We never saw the car coming at us. The impact of the crash sent me forward, crushing my boy's body between mine and the dashboard, killing him instantly. Please, tell your readers, never, never get into an automobile without putting their little ones in a car restraint seat." I never have, and hope and trust you won't either.

The lesson here is that great communicators add spice to their romancing efforts by stressing different forms of proof. Like any good courtship, varying the activities will keep the romance alive. In public speaking, the resulting effort will increase the audience's attention and interest level.

Audience-Friendly Courtship Tips

Later in the book, we will explore in greater depth the techniques for romancing a room and sustaining an audience's attention. Here are some tips to make your presentations more audience friendly and ensure that the speech will end at the same time for both you and your listeners:

- **Be aware of the audience's attention span at all times.**

- **Romance audiences with your own passion.** If you're not interested, how can you expect them to be?

- **Don't be boring.** Use a varied voice, with a varied presentation.

- **Involve the audience.** For example, use questions and answers.

- **Pose situations to audiences that are interesting to solve.** For example, the other day I heard someone say they were seventeen the day before yesterday, and the next year they will turn twenty years old. How can this be? (Answer: That person's birthday is on December 31, and the statement is made on January 1 of the next year.)

- **Tell engaging stories.** Get the audience to visualize what you're saying as you say it. Think of using a story or a visual illustration (visual aid) every sixty seconds in your presentation.

- **Say it simply.** If your listeners are confused or lost, they will quit paying attention immediately. When I go to see one of Shakespeare's plays, I always read the CliffsNotes in advance, so I don't get lost with the plot as I struggle with the language. This guarantees that I won't sleep through any parts of *King Lear*.

- **Eliminate attention distracters.** For example, never give a speech where there is a clock behind you. If there is, cover that clock so that the audience won't be tempted to look at the distraction. If someone comes into your room during a presentation, don't look at them and draw attention away from yourself; instead, move away from the door as they enter in order to bring the attention to you so as to distract from the distraction.

- **Don't be fixed in stone.** Be willing to adapt to changing circumstances, especially if you sense or learn that the audience's attention span is limited. Shorten the speech for a tired audience.

CHAPTER 5

Romance Anxiety

Human beings, like others in the animal world, suffer anxiety when they are in full and unprotected view of potential predators. We react to such a threat in the most primitive and understandable way: We can be overwhelmed with fear and a desire to flee the situation.

In romance, we call this anxiety about communicating with others shyness. Not surprisingly, in this age when we are increasingly able to avoid face-to-face interactions with others through the use of ATMs, the Internet, and telecommuting in our jobs, as many as 50 percent of all people in this country now refer to themselves as shy in nature.

Romancing others can be scary. When it came to asking a girl for a date as a youngster, I was much more of a retiring soul than a lothario. The story of my first official date proves it. As a sophomore class officer (in my all-boy high school), I needed to find a date for the Soph Hop Dance. I shared this dilemma with my then-freshman brother, Ray, who was outgoing and already well into the girls scene. Ray, who as an adult has not surprisingly become a highly successful salesman, told me it was easy—and he'd show me how. He asked me whom I'd select as my date, ideally. I told him I would ask Jeanie, but I was afraid she'd turn me down. "No problem," he responded.

Ray got her telephone number, dialed, and said, "Hey, Jeanie, this is Jim." Ray was now impersonating me. He had the smoothest conversation with her, asked her out (as me), and she responded that she'd be thrilled to go with him/me. With this hurdle out of the way, the date was a piece of cake.

Interactive anxiety is not limited to dating and romance. Rather, most people suffer some level of anxiety, or stage fright, any time they are exposed in full view before a group. Author Bernardo Carducci refers to this as the psychological rule of "salient objects"—meaning that it is human nature to scrutinize the most noticeable person in the room (e.g., the teacher, the soloist, the only woman) more critically than those who blend into the background. When laid so bare, we become self-conscious and fearful.

Every year in response to an opinion poll, Americans are asked what their greatest fear is. The respondents provide many expected answers: heights, spiders, flying, deep water, and enclosed spaces. In fact, in recent years, the *second* most common response is the fear of death. However, each year, the number one answer by a wide margin is the fear of speaking before a group.

When I recently shared these survey results with my speech class, I asked for reactions. One student raised her hand and provided this explanation as to why death only came in second: "If you're dead, you do not have to go before an audience and deliver a speech."

Another one of my students delivered a lighthearted speech titled "The Near-Speech Experience." In it, she said that just as there is a near-death experience (you know, the tunnel and the bright lights), there is also a near-speech experience. She described an experience she'd had two weeks earlier in the class: She was called on to speak, and felt a tingling sensation in her right arm. Soon, she felt as if she were floating outside her body observing it, and imagining she was in a cell with lots of other prisoners who were staring at her and wondering why no one had tried to escape. This was followed by a period of pitch black, lasting approximately two minutes, and about which she remembered nothing. Then suddenly, she was sitting in the classroom again hearing fellow students commenting about her vocal variety and topic selection. She realized that she had probably just given a speech.

If you have this fear of addressing a group, remember you are in good company. Legendary performers such as Barbra Streisand, Jimmy Stewart, Carol Burnett, Sir Laurence Olivier, and Liza Minnelli all admitted to a gripping fear and anxiety when performing before an audience. Andy Rooney, the glib commentator on *Sixty Minutes,* described this feeling as "public speaking, private agony."

The fear of communicating to a group is largely a learned anxiety. Recently, I was at San Francisco's Museum of Modern Art, where one of the exhibits was titled *The Fears Children Have.* The main graphic displayed a list of fears identified by numerous young children. They included such things as monsters under the bed, getting lost, falling off bicycles, rattlesnakes, and dragons. Tellingly, out of the ninety-eight kids questioned, not one mentioned anything about a fear of speaking before a group. The self-consciousness and anxiety associated with the otherwise natural act of talking to others is not an inborn trait. It is an *acquired* anxiety.

What is it, then, that causes the stage fright associated with communicating before others in a public setting? Why has the drug industry been able to make countless dollars selling pills directed at curbing phobias and panic attacks? What causes us to be flooded with anxiety and panic upon the mere mention that we have "to say a few words"? Recently, in an announcement publicizing a talk I gave about romancing the room, the sponsor of the event put at the bottom of the flyer: "This is not a workshop, and you will not be required to give a speech!" The sponsor was worried that even in that setting, if the attendees thought they'd be asked to speak, the attendance would suffer.

I suspect that the fear of communicating in a public setting has its genesis in two feelings: the fear of failure and the desire to avoid a negative evaluation by others.

As with other fears, speaking anxiety produces symptoms of nervousness such as sweaty palms, dry mouth, and shaking hands–all of which only further hamper clear communication.

Good communicators must learn to master their nervousness and anxiety. The following five simple steps will assist in freeing the speaker to romance the room with confidence.

1. Just Do It

The first step is to realize that the best cure is to speak and to speak regularly. Speaking is like physical exercise–you have to stick with it in order to stay in shape.

Make a commitment to start! Most people are forced into improving their communication abilities by having to make a presentation at work, giving a short speech at a school function, or presenting an award at a banquet.

But you can begin now by trying to improve every conversation. Be conscious of each word that you speak. Even your most relaxed conversations can become stepping-stones to reducing anxiety if you realize that every time you talk you are making a short presentation of sorts. When appropriate, try to insert your stories or parts of your presentation during your everyday conversations. This will help you with your sense of timing, and you will immediately see the reaction of the listener. Good communicators are constantly practicing on their unsuspecting listeners.

I try not to give any ad-lib speeches. Since I teach public speaking courses, I assume that at every event I attend—social or otherwise—I'm going to be asked to give a speech. I almost always have a speech prepared wherever I go. That way, I'm ready to practice my craft, and my audience won't be disappointed.

2. Identify Your Anxiety

The next step is to identify specifically the reason for your fear.

Once you have made a commitment to start romancing the room, you need to know why you are afraid. Let me give you an example. I hate flying! More specifically, I hate turbulence while flying! The actual acts of boarding a plane and flying to a destination don't bother me. But take me to thirty thousand feet and start bouncing around, and I become a nervous wreck. I think this anxiety is analogous to what most people experience when speaking in public.

When I analyzed my fear of flying, I learned that it wasn't flying as much as turbulence that bothered me. This was well proven when our family returned from a trip to Manhattan in the spring of 2000. We flew home out of the Newark airport. The flight proceeded smoothly for about forty-five minutes, then the pilot spoke over the intercom to explain that the plane was experiencing hydraulic anomalies and that we would be returning to

Newark to change equipment. We turned around and proceeded back.

As we awkwardly approached Newark, the pilot assured us that the numerous emergency vehicles lining the runway were just a safety precaution. This certainly didn't help to lower anyone's blood pressure.

After a rather hard landing, we deplaned and, within forty-five minutes, boarded another aircraft and took off for San Francisco a second time. The revealing part of this story is that the "hydraulic anomalies" didn't bother me nearly as much as the turbulence we experienced on the subsequent flight.

The lesson is clear: We need to determine what really is troubling us. Decide whether yours is a fear of failure, of speaking to strangers, or of speaking in public. Isolate your fear and try to address the precise reason why you are experiencing anxiety.

Try to find the source of your anxiety. My flying phobia developed after a bumpy trip to Denver, when my plane hit an air pocket and abruptly dropped what seemed to be thousands of feet. Several people were injured in the incident, and I have since been plagued with a strong apprehension of turbulence.

I have practiced, though, and I'm getting better. I even completed a three-day course in overcoming the fear of flying. I travel frequently and repeat my mantra that turbulence is "annoying but not dangerous!" Speaking in public definitely is not dangerous.

3. Visualize Success

The anxious would-be romancer should visualize success, remembering that audiences are almost always supportive and do not want speakers to fail. The speaker should create an image of the attentive listener, focused fastidiously on your every word.

What should you be saying to your listener that would create a favorable impression? Don't judge yourself on standards that are unobtainable. Don't believe that you immediately have to speak like Winston Churchill, John Kennedy, or Franklin Roosevelt in order to be a good speaker. Focus first on the results and how to get there, rather than the experience of actually making the presentation.

Frequently, individuals concentrate too much on the *how* of making their presentation and not on the *what* of the information being presented. Presumably, you are an expert in your own field, and that is why you have been asked to make a presentation. Be sure to review chapter 9, "The Classroom." If you are not an expert in the field, this presents a whole different set of problems that are discussed in chapter 12, "The Family Room."

You can reduce an enormous amount of nervousness by simply imagining you are talking to a good friend about your favorite topic. Be yourself! Relax! Practice with a friend. Cast off any contrary images. Don't worry about what you are not able to do; rather, concentrate on what you can accomplish.

4. Control the Signs of Nervousness

While you may not always be able to banish your nervousness completely, you can control the symptoms. Wipe your hands dry. Take a sip of water and a few deep breath before beginning to speak. Recognize that even the great public speakers have nervous energy before they speak— the difference is that they focus that energy into an enthusiastic presentation.

5. Practice, Practice

If you practice and practice some more, your level of confidence will increase.

This is different from number 1, "Just Do It." Once you have decided to start, you will need to practice. Practice with willing subjects in the actual room where you will be making your presentation so you get an advance sense of the distraction that the multiple eyes of the future audience will cause.

The more one communicates, the more fun it becomes. Romancing a room with success can generate an adrenaline rush that makes you want to repeat the experience over and over again. The audience will almost always react favorably to the techniques laid out in this book.

CHAPTER 6

The Five Imperatives of Romancing the Room

As a college speech teacher and a professional communicator, I have given and listened to tens of thousands of speeches. Each of these speeches was unique. However, there are some universal truths that allow you to distinguish communications that *soar* from those that *bore*. Communicators who desire to romance the room should come to view these truths as *imperatives*.

Like the fingers on a hand, there are five imperatives of romancing the room. The premise for each of these imperatives is that the listeners' attention is a precious commodity—hard to earn, and once lost not easily regained. Complying with these imperatives is the key to engaging and entertaining your audience.

Every time I communicate with others, I think of the scene in Woody Allen's *Annie Hall* in which subtitles rolled below the characters, reflecting what they were really thinking. I would pay a large sum of money to place a small CRT screen on the forehead of all listeners that could display their thought processes and reactions when I'm speaking. Since modern science has not yet devised such an interactive tool, following these five imperatives is the next best thing for ensuring you'll connect with others.

Imperative Number One: Romancing Means Never Having to Say You're Sorry

In the movie *Love Story*, Ali MacGraw's character is famous for telling Ryan O'Neal's character that "love means never having to say you're sorry." But when it comes to the way we communicate, we often do just the opposite: apologizing in advance while downplaying our communication skills. The first imperative emphasizes that such apologies reduce your communication effectiveness.

We frequently communicate in a self-deprecating way. For example, how many of us have given a gift and *before* the recipient even opened the package announced we "can take it back if it isn't right"? In the same vein, many times as my students hand in their term papers they confess to me: "It's not my best work." In both of these situations, the communicators downplay themselves in an effort to preempt any possible negative reaction.

Unfortunately, such apologies suggest to listeners that they should lower their expectations. It is not surprising, therefore, that when you make such apologies, it sends a message that the communication is not worthy of the listeners' attention or respect. It does not lead to successful romancing of the room.

Communicators no doubt reveal a lack of confidence in themselves and their messages when they consciously or subconsciously make such apologies. Apologetic communicators may harbor such a fear of failure or embarrassment that they ensure they'll be the first to give themselves the expected poor "grade."

Apologies can be either verbal or nonverbal. Here are some examples of verbal apologies.

THE EARLY EXCUSE

- "Please excuse me, this is the first time I have done this."
- "Sorry, I'm a bit disorganized this morning."
- "I accidentally left my notes at the office."
- "I didn't have much time to prepare for this."

THE GRADE YOURSELF AS YOU GO

- "This may not be the best example."
- "Maybe I didn't explain that very well."
- "I'm sorry if you can't see this transparency."

THE "PARDON ME" PRELIMINARY

- "This may not be right, but . . ."
- "I just did what I could . . ."
- "Well, I think this is . . ."
- "You may not agree with this, but . . ."

Nonverbal apologies also evidence themselves in varying ways.

THE MEA CULPA MIME

- Shrugging your shoulders
- Looking at your feet
- Shuffling your feet

THE CONFESSIONAL COUNTENANCE

- Rolling your eyes
- Grimacing (as if in pain)
- Laughing nervously at inappropriate times

THE UNDERSELLING VOICE PATTERN

- Delivering a declarative statement with vocal stress up at the end as if it were a question, as in "I want you to be home by

eleven o'clock?" versus "I want you to be home by eleven
o'clock!"

- Making a statement that is forceful on paper but delivered
  with a trembling or timid voice.

Grade Yourself an A

If you want to engage your listeners, then *positively* sell
yourself and your ideas. Avoid the verbal and nonverbal
apologies that lower expectations and reduce your credibility. The listeners want you to do well. They want you to
grade yourself an A from the start. They are anticipating
that your presentation will be provocative and entertaining. They certainly don't want to sit through a boring presentation full of apologies. If you are boring them, don't
make excuses for it; start applying good communication
techniques. You'll find your audience will be more recep-
tive and responsive.

If things really don't go as expected, *don't apologize–
improvise.* For example, on the weekend following the
terrorist attack on the World Trade Center we had five
families over for a comforting dinner. Bruce Bean's wife,
PJ, whispered to me that the occasion called for a "once in
a lifetime" presentation and prayer to bond our families.
No pressure! However, rather than decline or apologize, I
retreated to another room for five minutes, gathered my
thoughts, and grabbed the group photograph the families
had taken together during the previous holiday season. I
had my visual aid and my theme: like those in New York
City, we, too, had a picture to show others to illustrate what
really mattered.

There is one caveat to our first rule prohibiting those
underselling acts of contrition. There may be limited circumstances when to say you're sorry is an appropriate and

necessary action. An apology is in order if you have inadvertently caused harm (e.g., an unintended slight) or not completed some promise (e.g., you show up late).

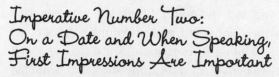

Imperative Number Two: On a Date and When Speaking, First Impressions Are Important

The first thirty seconds of any encounter are vitally important. Thinking about and then making a positive first impression are imperative if we want to romance persons and rooms with success.

Look in a Mirror

This lesson is not just for blind dates and job interviews. Before you communicate with others, think about the impression (physical and otherwise) you will make on your listeners. Is your hair out of place? Have your stockings run? Maybe there's something caught in your teeth, or it's *your* button-down collar that's at full staff. A look in the mirror (and attention to detail and basic fashion principles) will save you from the blind date failure.

Begin with a Bang

It is human nature that people's first impressions affect how they will view you and your message. So it is with communication. You must grab listeners' attention at the outset and have them form a positive first impression. Start out with an anecdote, a joke, a positive reference to the occasion or the audience, or some provocative bit of information. Wake up the listeners; pique their curiosity and win them over early. You must concentrate on pulling them out of their own problems, daydreams, or conversations. First impressions often are easy to read: If the listeners laugh, roar with approval, or seem physically and mentally engaged, you've got them.

Don't Start with a Whimper

Of course, you can violate the blind date imperative by starting not with a bang, but with a whimper. This could include a long-winded introduction, a disorganized preview of what's to come, or an unfunny story that is not tailored to your listeners. Or worse yet, you could start with a communication turnoff, such as an offensive statement or a negative comment that irritates your listeners.

When I'm pitching potential clients for business, the last thing I would do at the outset is tell them *how bad* I think their case seems or how I think their appearance will turn off any future jury. Rather, I romance them with enthusiasm and constructive analysis. I've learned the lesson that you must establish a favorable first impression and credibility if there's any hope of establishing a more long-term relationship.

Answer the Why of "Why Should They Listen to You?"

Once you have their attention, give the listeners a reason to keep listening. Make a promise of what your talk is going to do for them or what tantalizing information you are going to disseminate to them today. For example: "By the end of my talk today you will be able to . . ." Give them a reason to sustain their attention. Let your listeners know your speaking objectives.

Imperative Number Three: Romance the Fly

A friend of mine has an amazing skill. He can "romance a fly." Here's how he does it. He's in a room with a fly buzzing all about. He stands very still, makes eye contact with the fly, and virtually mesmerizes the insect. It lands, stops buzzing, and my friend approaches *slowly* with an open hand. He then gently closes his hand to capture the fly and transport it outdoors.

This skill provides us with the third imperative: You must romance the audience like a fly. Communicators must look their listeners in the eye, make Zen-like contact, and capture the listeners' attention with directness. The listeners will stop buzzing around physically and mentally, because now they're paying rapt attention to your message.

Make Zen-like Eye Contact

To romance the fly, you must obtain and maintain its attention. Nothing is more essential to this task than the imperative that you make eye contact with your listeners. This means capturing their attention without being overbearing. Do not just scan the audience without making direct contact with any one individual. Look directly at people, but do not stare them down.

Effective eye contact does *not* mean:

- *Eye-scanning*—that is, scanning without really looking at anyone
- *Staring* at listeners in a way that makes them feel uncomfortable and that their "space" has been invaded
- *False eye contact* such as looking over people's heads, making an S curve through the group, imagining they're all naked and not in the room as they really are, and so on

Rather, make friendly, engaging contact with as many people as possible. Connect with someone long enough that you can share a thought with that one person (and move on if you're speaking with more than one person).

The contact should be Zen-like in the sense that you are communicating directly and with your eyes.

Captivate Despite Distractions

Virtually every audience or set of listeners can be easily distracted. It is imperative that you eliminate distractions and focus on the communication between you as the sender and the listeners as the receivers. Take these commonsensical steps:

- **Eliminate distractions at the outset.** At the outset of your communication, look around the room and see if there are any objects or people that could distract your listeners. For example, a teacher should erase the chalkboard before going on to the next subject. Otherwise, students would have a tendency to look at matters that were no longer relevant.

- **Take the pause that refreshes.** When your listeners are all in a buzz or are talking among themselves, take a two-second pause, saying absolutely nothing. This has the effect of calming the room and focusing attention on the speaker, while the audience waits for what will happen next.

- **Eliminate distractions as you go.** This effort to direct the fly's attention as you go also requires the ongoing elimination of distractions. For example, the problem with distributing handouts during a presentation is that it is virtually impossible to prevent the listeners from reading ahead or focusing on something on paper that is not currently the subject of your communication.

- **Eliminate the nonverbal distractions.** As will be discussed in greater detail later in this book, you will distract your listeners if your body language or gestures are unnecessary or repetitive. Maybe it's a nervous fidget, playing with a pen while you speak, or engaging in some other distracting personal habit. The bottom line is that you cannot catch the fly if you flail around the room, swatting in wild attempts to get its attention.

Charismatic Capture without Killing

Romancing a fly (or your listeners) requires a degree of subtlety. Too many persons engage in "communication overkill." The presentation can be too loud, too repetitive, or too obvious. The listener, even if originally engaged, loses attention and begins to suffer from the wandering eye syndrome. My friend doesn't *kill* the fly, he captures it.

A classic example of communication overkill is the way many a frustrated parent has, at one time or another, interacted with his or her kids. They employ the "it's so because I say so" style without listening or attempting to engage the youngster in his or her own language. As described more fully in chapter 12, "The Family Room," parents need not give up authority in order to gain and sustain their children's attention. Romancing the family room, like any other, requires consideration of the listeners' interests as you mold your communications.

Move the Fly

Once you've got your listeners' attention, you must sustain and control it. In other words, once you've captured the fly, you must transport it to your chosen destination. This requires that the speaker define and make clear his or her specific objective. Generally, the speaker will ask the audience to learn, to be persuaded, or to be entertained.

Imperative Number Four: Add Spice to Your Romance Through Variety

The absolute nemesis to successful romancing is boredom. Thus, the fourth romancing the room imperative is that communicators must add spice to their relationship with listeners through variety. To combat potential monotony (and loss of attention), the speaker must offer variety to keep the romance in the relationship. Flat vocal patterns, a dry delivery, and tedious examples will deaden the communication relationship.

In later chapters, I will further explore the many specific secrets to keeping the romance alive by incorporating variety in every sense. But for now, start thinking of these quick tips to spice up your speeches:

VARIETY IN VOCAL PATTERNS
- Inflection
- Rate
- Pause
- Volume
- Pitch

VARIETY IN SUPPORTING MATERIALS
- Stories
- Quotations
- Common allusions
- Novel information
- Analogies and similes
- Imagery

VARIETY IN REQUESTED REACTIONS

- Laughter
- Suspense
- Irony
- Poignancy
- Fear
- Curiosity

Bottom line—you can and must strive for variety in order to keep the romance in your communications. Such variety will produce a kaleidoscope of reactions. Spice it up and keep your listeners leaning in to catch your every word.

Imperative Number Five: End Before Expected: The Premature Evacuation

The listeners' response to a communicator often depends on final impressions as well. Certainly, you want to guarantee they don't stop listening before you stop talking! To increase your odds of success at achieving a romancing communication, you must engage in a "premature evacuation"—that is, end before they expect you to end . . . *always!*

Know Time Expectations

Listeners have preexisting expectations as to the length of your presentation. If you are expected to speak for one hour, end your talk in fifty-five minutes. By the same token, if they expect your presentation to last ten minutes, end it short of the anticipated length. If you're giving a lecture to your teenager, make your main points but don't commit overkill by repeating them endlessly.

There can be a large penalty for going overtime. No mat-

ter how good you have been, the listeners get the feeling
that the presentation is going on too long. They look at
their watches. Now, rather than earning favorable impressions, you risk a negative review because it dragged on.

Conversely, the reward for ending early can be palpable.
The listeners feel as if school got out early, and they appre-
ciate your timing. Their attention spans, not yet ready to
shut off, are still operating on all cylinders. If you're lucky,
they'll leave with their engines revved up, still engaged and
fully romanced.

Recently, I experienced firsthand the benefits of ending
early. I was asked to address a committee, chaired by
former Supreme Court Justice Byron White, that was con-
sidering whether to realign our federal courts. The committee scheduled some forty-five ten-minute speeches for a
single day, running from 9:00 A.M. to 5:00 P.M. Unfortunately, I was given the final slot at 4:50 P.M. I spoke for precisely four and a half minutes. Thereafter, I announced
with good humor that I was aware that the average adult
attention span was seven minutes. I sympathized with the
committee for having been there all day and gracefully
concluded my remarks. I received a standing ovation from
Justice White and his grateful colleagues!

Be Ever Aware of Listeners' Attention Spans

The bottom line is that you must constantly be aware of
your listeners' attention spans. Don't overstay your welcome; keep them romanced throughout your communication. If you follow the five imperatives, you'll succeed every
time!

FIVE IMPERATIVES CHECKLIST

1. **NEVER HAVING TO SAY YOU'RE SORRY: NO APOLOGIES**
   - Are you making verbal or nonverbal apologies as you communicate?
   - Are you able to improvise if something doesn't go as planned?
   - Have you prepared well enough?
   - Do you have backup if there are technical difficulties?

2. **ON A DATE AND WHEN SPEAKING, FIRST IMPRESSIONS ARE IMPORTANT**
   - Have you looked in the mirror?
   - Do you have a good opening?
   - Can you answer the why of "why should they listen to you?"

3. **ROMANCE THE FLY: MAKE CONNECTIONS**
   - Are you making eye contact with your listeners?
   - Have you eliminated distractions?

4. **ADD SPICE TO YOUR ROMANCE THROUGH VARIETY**
   - Do you have enough variety in your communication?
   - Is your voice in a monotone?
   - Do you have good examples and stories?

5. **END BEFORE EXPECTED: PREMATURE EVACUATION**
   - How much time are you allotted?
   - How long is your listeners' attention spans?
   - Are you ending before they expect you to end?

PART 2

Romancing Each and Every Room

CHAPTER 7

The Sales Room

You may think that persuasion is only for ancient Greeks and modern speech geeks; a traditional form of public speaking where you stand and discourse eloquently at a podium, persuading people to agree with your views on some controversial topic. This certainly is a part of persuasion, but only a small part.

Persuasion is the ability to move someone from one set of attitudes, behaviors, or beliefs to another set of attitudes, behaviors, or beliefs. Persuasion and the art of the sale can mean both swaying listeners and reinforcing their ideas and practices. For example, attempting to keep someone voting in your favor, or ensuring that someone can resist others who later come up with counterideas, are considered forms of selling as well.

The art of persuasion, of making the sale, may be the communication form most analogous to romance. For romance is a series of acts that persuade someone you like to like you. If you think otherwise, just read the personals ads of any newspaper's classified section: "Attractive, slim, fun-loving SWF who enjoys dancing and healthy activities seeks NSM for meaningful relationship." Romantic overtures, whether by a personal ad, a glance across the room, or an arranged meeting through friends, are a form of *selling* oneself to another person.

Appeals to Values

Let's take the broad example of someone who persuades for a living: a telemarketer. The telemarketer is trying to persuade you to give money to some charity or to switch phone services. Like any good communicator, he or she wants to get your attention. That's the number one rule of communication. Persuasion is no different; first you must get your audience's attention.

When telemarketers call, they say, "How are you doing tonight?" because they want to engage you. They want you to say something. They're hoping the response to "How are you?" is not "Quit bothering me–" CLICK. They want to focus your attention and engage. One of the things you must do in persuading is get attention and immediately engage.

You then have to identify what the resistance points are. What's the resistance to a telemarketer? You don't want to part with your money. You don't want to be bothered. So the telemarketer, the persuader, needs to identify the positive or negative values that will help persuade you to contribute to his or her cause. Some books call this value orientation. When people call me asking for money for police charities, they refer to concepts like protection, safety, security, and community. These are positive values–again, the idea is to link the pitch with values the caller thinks you will see as positive. In the alternative, sometimes callers will associate their ideas with the avoidance of negative values. What are negative values for the police charity? Crime, violence, fear, guilt . . . In either event, the telemarketer orients you toward or away from selected values to enhance the sale.

Setting the Thesis

You cannot select the values supporting your appeal unless you first clearly define the goal of your persuasive communication. In the vernacular, this means simply: What's your point? If you cannot answer this question in advance of your effort to sell your idea, then you can hardly achieve your objective.

In a formal presentation, the speaker must set forth the persuasive thesis at the outset of the speech immediately following the introduction. This "thesis setting" section of the presentation should be concise and unmistakable, followed by a preview of the reasons and examples that will prove the thesis. If the length of an ideal introduction does not exceed 10 percent of the total presentation, the thesis setting section that follows should be even more succinct.

Say, for example, you are attempting to persuade a group of computer-phobic elder citizens to buy personal computers because e-mail access can enhance their lives. After you get their attention with a catchy introduction, you set your thesis: A personal computer is an excellent investment because it provides access to e-mail communications with friends and family. You then preview your supporting points: (1) E-mail on personal computers is easy to learn, (2) e-mail communications are like personal letters with instant transmission and response, and (3) you can increase the frequency of connecting with friends and family—who are most likely already online.

Once you have set the thesis in your persuasive communication, you go about making your appeal. In our e-mail presentation, for example, these points no doubt would include references to the positive values of staying in touch, getting the benefits of instant access to information, maintaining family harmony, and achieving an immediate return on the investment in the computer. On the other side, the communicator could, if appropriate, highlight the negative values of being anachronistic, disconnected, and penurious.

Organizing the Body of the Presentation

Once you have set the thesis of your argument, you go to the body of the speech or sales presentation. This is where the speaker makes the main points and supports them with arguments and proofs. The communicator's objective is to move the audience to the desired attitude, behavior, or belief.

When creating the body of a persuasive presentation, most speakers will brainstorm to identify the major points supporting the thesis. Your challenge is to organize these points into an outline that will represent the body of the speech. This outline often will be predicated on an "importance sliding scale," with the points addressed from the least persuasive to the most persuasive ("ascending order"), or from the most persuasive to the least persuasive ("descending order").

For example, let us imagine the following thesis statement: Cell phones should not be allowed in automobiles. The ascending order of points might be: (1) cell phone communications while driving are ineffective due to distractions, (2) such communications disturb the benefits of privacy unique to driving, and (3) the distractions of talking on a cell phone while driving can lead to accidents and serious injuries to the driver and others. You could use an ascending order when it is deemed important to build to the biggest point. This might be effective when, for example, the audience is uninitiated or seemingly supportive, such that it will be patient, waiting for the biggest point at the end with the most lasting effect.

On the other hand, a speaker might outline the points of the thesis in a descending order, starting with the critically important danger issue. When an audience is potentially hostile to the thesis or might be impatient or tired, the speaker may be compelled to hit the biggest point first. Rather than building to a conclusion, the speaker follows the lead point with the others by saying that the other points, when taken together, cumulatively demonstrate that the listeners should be moved to agree.

As an attorney, I make these organizational decisions in every trial. It is called the ordering of witnesses. Do I lead with my star witness because I want my client's case to gain immediate and hopefully irreversible momentum? Or do I build to a crescendo so that the jury has the strongest point most recently in mind? As with specches, the answer is that it depends on the mood of the audience.

Of course, using romance techniques when "selling" your thesis is not removed from what one does during the process of courting. You plan your dates with the person who is the object of your ardor, sometimes trying to knock his or her socks off at the beginning to solidify your chances. Other times, you build slowly, starting with coffee, then lunch, then the fancy dinner. Persuasion in group and sales settings is no different.

Certainly, however, you should not organize and outline your points randomly or chaotically. So many speakers present their points by way of *listing* them, rather than by developing the points (e.g., "my first point, my second point, my third point," etc.). Ask yourself this: If you could rearrange the points randomly, would the speech be unaffected? If so, then the speech is not purposefully organized, but rather accidentally and potentially less effective. Test your outline by asking *why* each point follows the other, and include transitions that make the structure clear to the listeners.

The outline for a persuasive speech often follows one of two overall patterns: (1) the problem-solution approach, or (2) the motivational sequence. Presenters use both these organizational patterns depending upon the circumstances of the speech.

Problem-Solution Approach

The body of this type of persuasive speech is organized around two principal points: the problem and the solution. After introducing the speech and setting the thesis, the speaker communicates to the audience that there is a problem facing them or society at large. The speaker might first need to persuade the listeners that there is, in fact, a problem. This could require presentation of facts concerning its existence and magnitude, as well as showing why it is of immediate concern to this group of listeners. The speaker then presents points demonstrating that the problem is significant and, if not addressed, could have devastating and harmful consequences.

Having established the existence and significance of the problem, the speaker then addresses his or her proposed solution. The solution points demonstrate why the solution will work and the benefits to be gained if it is implemented. If there are potential downsides to implementing the solution (e.g., costs, delay, etc.), the speaker must be prepared to show that these downsides are outweighed by the benefits. The speaker often concludes a problem-solution speech with a call to action.

The problem-solution approach is a straightforward organizational pattern for persuasive presentations on matters of policy, personal behavior, and other concrete topics. Politicians who are making presentations on pending or proposed legislation typically will employ this outline approach.

Motivational Sequence

The motivational sequence, first devised by Alan H. Monroe at Purdue University, is an organizational pattern premised on the audience's psychological reaction to points of persuasion. The sequence includes these steps: (1) attention, (2) need, (3) satisfaction, (4) visualization, and (5) action. Essentially, the speaker organizes the presentation by first getting the *attention* of the listeners on the chosen topic. Then the speaker highlights that the audience has a *need* in the sense that the status quo is lacking on some essential matter. Then come points showing that the need can be *satisfied* by taking some step to fulfill it. The speaker then asks the audience to *visualize* its situation once the need is satisfied—visually associating the situation in positive terms. Finally, the speaker exhorts the listeners to take a specific *action* to satisfy the identified need.

This motivational sequence underlies much of the persuasion that takes place on a daily basis when a salesperson attempts to convince a customer to buy a product. For example, let's examine a hypothetical salesperson attempting to sell a wireless computer network system to a business consumer. First, the salesperson must, through an advertisement, lead, or other contact, get the *attention* of the customer. As they say, you have to get their attention so you can get your foot in the door. Once the customer is paying attention, the salesperson highlights the *need* to have computers linked one to the other, and the difficulties and expense associated with the company's present wired connections. As part of this sales call, perhaps using visual aids, examples, and testimonials, the sales rep shows how installation of a wireless computer network at the business will directly *satisfy* its need, that is, to eliminate the costs and inconveniences of the present wiring (and in the long run actually pay for the new system itself). The salesperson now asks him or her to *visualize* the benefit of using this system at the customer's place of business: happy and more productive workers who won't be calling for outside computer help as before. Finally, the salesperson must close the deal by asking the customer to take *action*—in this case agreeing to the purchase (and no doubt committing to it by signing a contract and making a first installment payment).

The motivational sequence describes the organizational pattern used in most sales situations and in speeches requiring the psychological agreement of the audience. Appropriately enough, motivational speakers frequently employ this pattern, reminding themselves to touch each of the motivational bases along the way.

Supporting the Points of Persuasion

It is not enough that you make points and present arguments in a persuasive speech. To romance the sales room effectively you must support these arguments with logic, ethics, and emotion. We learned earlier that such "proofs" are referred to as logos, ethos, and pathos.

In many a romance, the person being courted will say, "Don't just talk . . . show me that you love me." The same is true in persuasive speaking. The listeners don't want to hear just the abstract points and arguments behind a request that they change their attitudes, behaviors, or beliefs. They want evidence and examples showing that it is the right step for them to take.

The evidence or proof that supports a persuasive argument often consists of points of logic. An argument will be described as supporting certain logical inferences, and the speaker will set forth such logic to persuade the audience that the point is well taken. In courts of law, we are most familiar with this form of logical proof; say, for example, when the jury is told to convict because a defendant has no alibi for the time and date of the crime.

When I'm attempting to persuade juries of the correctness of my client's position in a case, I also support the points of persuasion with the ethical strength of a witness or supporting fact. If, say, the expert has a Nobel Prize in chemistry, it is far more likely that his or her testimony in my product liability case (e.g., "the hip replacement device came apart due to a breakdown in the adhesive polymers used by the medical supply company") is going to be persuasive. It won't hurt if I sound like I know what I'm talking about as well (and that I can pronounce the complex terms correctly).

As we saw earlier, the term "emotional proof" is no oxymoron. You can support the points of persuasion and argument made in the body of a presentation by using supporting materials and examples that appeal to the audience's emotions. For example, Franklin Roosevelt may have tried for months and years logically to persuade Americans that the Nazi advances in Europe must be halted. However, it was the combined effect of the emotions of fear, anger, and national pride that made the response to the December 7, 1941, attack on Pearl Harbor so overwhelming and unanimous.

The speaker's detailed outline should include not only the main points, but also the supporting proofs as well. There is a large reservoir of such supporting materials, be they facts, personal stories, quotations, or anecdotes. Moving an audience to a desired thesis requires constant use of these tools.

Techniques for Overcoming Obstacles and "Sales Resistance"

As salespersons, persuasive speakers, and any person seeking to woo a lover will tell you, they are often met with resistance in the process. The way to achieve success in romancing the sales room, therefore, lies in identifying the obstacles to success and using the techniques for overcoming them.

As mentioned in earlier chapters, speakers must always know the audience in order to understand what obstacles they will face in the sales room. Who's out there? What do they know and what do they value or detest? What are their resistance points to the particular problem/need or solution/action step in a particular presentation? Knowing the answer to these questions and the hurdles they might erect can shape the selection of supporting materials and techniques necessary to overcome them.

There are several potent persuasive techniques for overcoming audience obstacles. The first is called *identification*. Effective communicators look to use language, ideas, and supporting methods with which the listeners can identify. You look for common ground that you and the audience share, a harmony of ideas. This technique works very well in a hostile audience setting, one in which people disagree with you at the beginning. In my speech class, I sometimes give a hostile audience assignment; for example, you might have to give a speech on pro-choice to a right-to-life organization. In that kind of circumstance, you need to find common ground—often called the "yes-yes" method.

If I really have a hostile audience, before I even get to a

yes on ideas I have to get to a yes on me. I've got to get the listeners to like me. So I start off telling them a story about my family or something else personal, to make them warm up to me. Several studies show that if you like the speaker, you'll usually like his or her ideas. As a speaker, you need to get the audience to like you, then like your idea.

Let's try an example. One time I had to give a speech advocating amnesty for those who avoided the Vietnam War to a Veterans of Foreign Wars (VFW) group. I was definitely facing a hostile audience. These veterans undoubtedly believed that people who avoided their military obligations were avoiding their responsibility as citizens. I had a problem, so I didn't start off right in their face, or they would have rejected me and my argument.

I looked for common ground, or a point of identification—in this case, a common theme of constitutional rights. You see, these veterans had fought, and their friends had died, to preserve our constitutional freedoms, *including* the right to dissent. They were fighting for values we all share. That's the yes-yes argument. We agreed that the Constitution of this country is worth fighting for, including its protections for people who have different, even radical, ideas. I was saying that we shared a love of the Constitution. If you love the right to express your ideas, you must support the right of others to exercise their beliefs, even if you disagree with their point of view.

Once I'd found the common ground, I then made the transition from the idea we shared, the right to dissent, to the idea I wanted the audience to accept—amnesty. Do you think that by the end of the speech all the veterans believed that amnesty should be given to those who avoided Vietnam? No. We agreed to disagree on the large subject, but we could agree that these are people of good conscience that made this decision.

Another persuasive technique is *direction*. This is simply telling your audience what you want them to do. Let me give you an example: You're interviewing for a job. You could tell the interviewer exactly what you want him or her to do: "I want you to hire me." Direction is literally telling a person what you want him or her to do.

When I'm in a trial, I give direction to the jury. I say, "This is what I want you to do. You're going to get a little form, and there will be a box for the plaintiff, my client, and one for the defendant. What I want you to do is check the verdict box for the plaintiff. Then where it has a dollar sign next to a long line, I want you to use as much of that line as possible, with as many zeros as possible. I want you to write on that line one point nine million dollars. That's one, comma, nine zero zero, comma, zero zero zero, point, zero zero." Literally giving direction.

Now you have to be careful in giving direction, because you can only go so far before your direction starts to sound condescending. If you play it out too much, people may feel like you're selling them. That might be a case when you use *suggestion* rather than direction. What's the power of suggestion? What if I said to you, "Go open the door and let some air in here?" That's direction. Now, I could say the same thing using suggestion: "It sure is hot in here." I suggest the action you should take. If I have an audience that is resistant to direction, I use suggestion.

Perhaps the most important technique for romancing the sales room is to *read the audience's mind*. Now, this is not possible in a literal sense, although with advance information about the audience and by reading its reactions while you're speaking, you can come pretty close.

The reason why it is so important to read your audience's mind while trying to persuade it is that you can adapt your presentation in progress. In romance and courting, we have long understood what this is all about: You might be with the person of your intended affection and saying something or suggesting a future activity that—if you could read minds—would be the death knell to the relationship (e.g., mentioning your love of George W. Bush to a die-hard Democrat, suggesting a hot-air balloon ride to someone with a fear of heights, or offering an alcoholic beverage to a teetotaler). If you only knew!

Reading an audience (and doing good advance work before speaking) allows you to make adjustments that will help you make the sale. One of the biggest adjustments you can make is to decide if you must include *counterpersuasion* to rebut what the audience is thinking as you are making your points. Counterpersuasion means expressly acknowledging the argument or arguments that are in opposition to your thesis, and then rebutting them in your speech itself.

The tough part is knowing whether the audience members are actually formulating the counterarguments while you are speaking. If they are, you can preempt the arguments in your speech and possibly douse the fire of dissent before it runs rampant on its own. For example, if you're attempting to persuade an audience that school uniforms should be required even at public schools in order to provide discipline, you could anticipate that members of the audience might self-generate the opposition point that such a rule interferes with freedom of expression and attire. In such a situation, you could use counterpersuasion by saying, "Some people might argue that this proposition violates the free expression rights of students, but to that I say that such expression is hardly 'free' because it is only the children of the rich who can even afford to purchase such diverse wardrobes in the first place."

Counterpersuasion is important not only when listeners

generate such ideas on their own; it is also a useful technique to inoculate them from such arguments if they are exposed to them in the future. Of course, if the listeners will neither formulate the counterpoint on their own nor be exposed to it in the future, you risk planting a seed of doubt that never would have sprouted at all. Thus, knowing and reading your audience becomes even more critical.

Reading an audience is also vitally important if you are addressing a narrow point of persuasion that does not seem to affect listeners' interests directly. In such situations, it is often useful to use a technique known as *broadening*. As a speaker, you acknowledge that your topic addresses a fairly narrow subject; however, you then emphasize that the values underlying or affected by the persuasive point are broader and will affect interests that are of concern to your listeners.

For example, many of my students over the years have spoken on the subject of animal testing. Occasionally, the class of Stanford undergraduates could seemingly care less about the fate of lab rats or abstract rules governing animal testing. However, the effective speakers in such situations use the broadening technique. These students state that they are not simply talking about animal rights or arcane testing procedures; rather, they are addressing a concern with far broader implications (e.g., "the ability of scientists to conduct tests to find cures for diseases" or "the respect we give to other species in and out of the laboratory, endangered and otherwise").

Of course, the ultimate form of persuasion, and one that also derives from reading the audience's mind, is when you can persuade the listeners to persuade themselves. I have long referred to this as the *O. Henry technique*. The author O. Henry was famous for his short stories, which had a revealing twist at the end. For example, there was "The

Ransom of Red Chief," in which the criminals kidnapped a child whose behavior was so awful that they kept *lowering* the ransom demand, to the point of offering the parents money to take the brat back!

In public speaking, it is a rare and truly marvelous moment when the same twist can be applied to an audience. In 1968, at the height of the dissent over the Vietnam War, the speech that won the national high school championship was by a young man who used the technique of presenting the first-person view of a soldier in that war. He said that the war was controversial and he didn't want to fight it, but his family at home strongly wanted him to fulfill his duty. Although he fought in this jungle war, he felt it was an endless struggle with no clear outcome. He wondered if he would ever see his wife and children again. And, by the way, his name was Nguyen van Pang, and he was a North Vietnamese soldier! The speaker's point was not, as the audience may have assumed, that for America this was an awful ordeal, but rather that in war we regrettably dehumanize "the enemy" as a means of waging war. With the aid of the O. Henry technique, the audience personalized the persuasive point from its own unguided reaction.

PERSUASION REVIEW QUESTIONS

1. Persuasion requires the ability to do what? _____

2. What is the number one rule of all communication? _____

3. What is the importance of determining resistance points? _____

4. What is the importance of a clear thesis setting in your speech?

5. What must you use to persuade someone? _____
_____

6. Why is broadening an effective persuasive technique? _____
_____

7. Once you've determined the problem and the solution of your speech, what must follow at the end of the speech? _____

8. Why is it important to know your audience? _____
_____

9. Name four persuasive techniques. _____
_____

ANSWERS TO PERSUASION REVIEW QUESTIONS

1. The ability to move someone from one set of attitudes, feelings, and beliefs to another set of attitudes, feelings, and beliefs.

2. You have to get your listeners' attention.

3. They allow you to appeal to positive and negative values.

4. It makes the purpose of your speech clear to your audience.

5. Arguments and proofs.

6. Because it allows you to appeal to general values in order to persuade someone.

7. An action step.

8. Knowing your audience helps you to determine its positive and negative values.

9. Identification, direction, suggestion, and counterpersuasion.

PERSUASION SPEECH CHECKLIST

BEFORE THE SPEECH
Who is my audience? _____
_____

What are the main resistance points of the audience? _____
_____

What are the positive values of the audience? _____

_____

What are the negative values of the audience? _____

_____

How long do I want my speech to be? _____

INTRODUCTION
What is the thesis of my speech? _____

_____

What do I want to accomplish in terms of persuading the audience? _____

_____

BODY
What arguments will you use? _____

_____

_____

_____

What kinds of proofs will you use? _____

_____

_____

_____

What persuasive techniques should you use? _____

_____

_____

CHAPTER 8

The Money Room

When my local Catholic priest, Father Michael, approached me at the annual Christmas pageant, I knew I was in trouble. Father Michael is a consummate room romancer. He freely admits to being in "marketing for God." He seldom forgets a name and greets everyone with an enthusiastic handshake and a warm pat on the back. At times, meeting Father Michael on the street seems like a reunion with a long-lost battle companion you have not spoken to in decades. Understand, Father Michael does this with a genuine love of people at heart; you never feel that he is patronizing or disingenuous. There is no doubt Father Michael is a very likable soul.

The night of the Christmas pageant Father Michael followed his usual format—the handshake, the exchange of pleasantries, and the query about the health of the family. Then he asked in his amiable Irish accent, "So, Jimmy boy, have ya heard about the archdiocese's Campaign for Catholic Education?" Without pausing for me to answer, he went on. "The bishop is trying to establish a thirty-million-dollar endowment fund to help families in need provide a Catholic education for their children. It's a great

program. Will you give us a hand in recruiting a few people to help in the fund-raising effort?"

Now, I must admit I did say that I would help by giving
some speeches to rally the troops. I always have time to
stand in front of an audience for a worthwhile cause. However, I don't remember volunteering to be the chairman of
the recruiting committee, a title that appeared in the first
letter sent to the parish regarding the campaign, but Father Michael has a way of transposing mild expressions of
interest into leadership positions. Fortunately, the campaign was a perfect laboratory for testing some *Romancing
the Room* communication formulas.

The campaign needed to convey a clear message and
a request for money to approximately eighteen hundred
families. The message ultimately came down to a simple
request for people to dig into their pockets and give money
to a cause that would not benefit them personally in any
way . . . other than the warm feeling they got from knowing
they were helping those less fortunate than themselves.

At every level, *Romancing the Room* techniques needed to
be deployed. In order to get this message to the parish-
ioners, we needed to train approximately one hundred vol-
unteers to communicate effectively and personably with
large audiences, in small meetings, and person-to-person,
using techniques ranging from telephone calls to voice
mail, letters, and e-mails.

The first opportunity to test my theories came with the
initial meeting of the steering committee. It was an inauspi-
cious start. There was no agenda, a lot of idle chatter, and no
one seemed to be in charge—except Father Michael, who
was happy to let things take a rather random course. Fortunately, our appointed and tireless fund-raising chairwoman
saved the day by taking over the meetings.

Run Meetings Efficiently

One of the largest complaints I hear from people in every walk of life, from both for-profit and nonprofit environments, is the frustration of having to participate in ineffectively run meetings. *Don't waste people's time.* This is particularly important when people are volunteering their time and talent. If you learn nothing else from this book, learn how to conduct an effective meeting and how to be an invigorating participant if you are not the leader. Remember—a date won't be a success if you don't have a plan *and* show up on time. The same proves true here.

Since most romancing efforts—including asking for money—take place as part of presentations at meetings, it is important to understand that there is no bigger turn-off than a poorly run meeting. There is a reason why, as Meeting Professionals International estimates, some $40 billion is spent each year on meeting-related expenditures. The meeting or conference should be well-organized, entertaining, and helpful to its participants.

We all know what bad meetings are, but do you know what makes a good meeting? There are seven imperatives to running an effective meeting.

1. **Start and end on time!** Don't wait for everyone to get there. People are perpetually late, but they will stop being late to your meetings if they know you are always prompt and willing to start without them. Introduce everyone that is there, and try to introduce each person as he or she comes into the meeting.

2. **Have a written agenda.** Establish why you're here, where you're going, and how long you think it will take to cover each topic. Even if you are covering only one or two topics, write them down and pass out agendas to

everyone. If handing out written agendas is impractical, then verbally go over the agenda or have it available on a chalkboard, a chart, or a computer program.

3. **Make the meeting engaging.** If you are covering the boring details of your budget, spice it up! Don't get carried away, but do something novel to add a little life to what would normally be a dull topic. People will come to your meeting with more enthusiasm if they know it will be engaging and entertaining.

4. **Focus.** The biggest challenge to running an effective meeting is keeping the group focused on the agenda. When a meeting has no clear leader, goals, or agenda, the discussions tend to veer off target. Good leaders and participants must learn how to politely table or postpone discussions of unrelated or distracting topics.

5. **Understand the dynamics of the group.** It often happens that quiet people can offer significant contributions to a meeting, while vocal types may add the least to the productivity of the group.

6. **End before expected.** Always try to end early. Meetings inevitably drag on much too long. Ending a meeting before expected will surprise and delight all participants.

7. **Take charge!** Don't let the meeting flounder just because you're not the leader. Take some initiative! You don't have to be a domineering, egotistical control freak to help facilitate a better meeting. Subtle suggestions and nonthreatening questions can move a meeting from deadly dull to fascinating. Here are a few examples:

- "Have we put together an agenda for this meeting yet?"
- "Could the two of you finish that discussion later and report back to us?"

- "Before we spend more time discussing that issue, could we finish with the remaining items on the agenda?"

Fund-Raising: The Basic Steps

When you are attempting to romance the money room, you apply the most fundamental principle of romance itself: long-distance relationships almost never work. You simply cannot make the vital connection by e-mail or other means of correspondence. A successful romance ultimately requires person-to-person contact. And so does raising money.

The essence of any fund-raising effort is to connect personally with others and to personalize the appeal. There's a reason why direct-mail marketing efforts–no matter how well-researched and targeted–produce only a 1 to 2 percent response rate. There is no personal connection and no one present to overcome the many obstacles that arise when people are asked to give money. Cold calls from telemarketers don't fare any better for the same reason: There is no bond of any kind between caller and recipient.

As in many of our other romancing venues, the money room offers challenges because the listeners have both expressed and unstated reasons to resist the communication. In this setting, such points of resistance are not hard to identify: short attention spans ("I don't have time right now"), a lack of money ("Things are very tight right now for us"), and alternatives ("I already gave at the office").

To overcome these obstacles, the money room romancer must make a personalized connection and find ways to convince the potential contributor to fall in love with the cause. Thus, the communicator must both connect with the contributor and connect the contributor to the values and objects of the fund-raising project itself.

In order to make a personal connection to a potential contributor, the fund-raiser must use the now-established romance technique: learn about the audience in order to make your connection more engaging. Oftentimes, particularly in smaller fund-raising efforts (e.g., selling raffle tickets for the local Little League), you will already know a great deal about the group from whom you're soliciting. This gives you an immediate connection and points upon which to build, such as knowing their anticipated level of giving and the types of appeal that will be most successful.

When, as is often the case, you do not personally know the potential donor, it is difficult to fathom what his or her giving capacity might be. Perhaps that person has recently invested well, received some lucrative stock options, or inherited money from a long-lost aunt. It is hard to keep track of all these possibilities. However, you can often learn this type of information in small, informal meetings with a select group of well-connected individuals. These quasi-social gatherings have two objectives: to introduce the project to a number of potential donors, and to estimate how much other prospective donors may be able to contribute to the cause. This information would be kept confidential and recorded on a chart similar to the one below.

NAME	POTENTIAL CONTRIBUTION	COMMENTS
Jane Doe, John Doe		
Mary Ham, Joe Giles		
Leo Smith		
Etc. . . .		

After introducing the project to the group and answering any questions, hand out the list to each person and have her or him spend a few minutes running through it and writing in their estimates of potential contribution amounts. Add any comments about the listed person's ability to contribute.

The techniques of *Romancing the Room* are particularly important when teaching others how to solicit money. Here are the three steps to assist others in coming to the money room.

Step One: Visualize the Goal

Open the meeting by introducing everyone. Then verbally describe the wonderful feeling each of them potentially will have in accomplishing the group's objective, whether it is opening the doors to a new gymnasium, helping families in need to get a better education, or having your first meeting at your new local community center. I do not believe in overhyping people with unrealistic visualizations. Just a simple appreciative statement that clearly defines what you want to accomplish will help your solicitors to feel, will help them to glean a little of the passion for the goal. Use all your romancing abilities to translate what you see into the minds of the committee.

These romancing principles are now familiar:

- Make a good first impression.
- Don't apologize about asking for money.
- Keep your listeners' attention.
- Spice up your presentation with variety.
- End before expected!

Step Two: Make the First Call for an Appointment

The most critical part of the solicitation process is the first call. With the number of telemarketing calls that we all receive these days, it is imperative not to have your first call be a telephone solicitation; it should instead be a request to meet the party you are calling to explain a little bit about the project. The objective is not to ask for money over the telephone.

We're not talking about cold calls. Rather, the romance technique capitalizes on what is referred to as a "warm call," in which there is some connecting point between the caller and the potential contributor as a result of their association through a group, a community, or an activity. In this situation, the first sentence out of your mouth during the first call might be something like:

"This is [your name], calling on behalf of [your group] to talk about [your project]. I would like to get together with you for about fifteen minutes to discuss this project with you. Do you perhaps have time next Wednesday night at about 7:30?"

It is critical to look at your calendar and find some available times when you can meet with these people before you call. It is much more difficult to establish the first appointment if you use an open-ended question. Do not ask: "Is there a time we could get together and discuss this?" Establish times when you are available first.

Step Three: What to Say and How to Close

First off, thank the potential contributor for taking time to meet with you. Second, ask how much time you have. You need to adjust your presentation to his or her needs and time frame. You may have ten minutes, or you may have thirty minutes. It is critical to adjust your presentation if necessary. Remember the fifth imperative of good romancing: always end before expected, regardless of how much time you have.

Generally, people like to start out with a little small talk: perhaps modest compliments about their home, or maybe

comments about some interesting piece of clothing, the
weather, the children, the grandchildren, health issues, or
current events. Small talk is great for breaking the ice on
the first dates and when soliciting. It helps you get comfortable with someone. The key to small talk is to focus on asking questions of the potential contributors. *Do not* spend
the whole time talking about yourself. This would lead to a
disastrous date—and a bored potential donor. A little bit of
back-and-forth swapping of information is good. Ideally,
you would concentrate on letting your potential contributor
talk. Thus far the conversation might look like this:

> **SOLICITOR:** "Thanks for taking time to meet with us
> about [the project]. How much time do we have?"

> **PROSPECT:** "Well, I have about thirty minutes before I
> need to help the kids get off to bed."

> **SOLICITOR:** "Great. How are your kids doing?"

> **PROSPECT:** "They're fine. Richard is growing up so
> quickly. He'll be in seventh grade next year. How are
> your kids doing?"

> **SOLICITOR:** "They're fine. Megan is headed to high
> school and Michael is trying to figure out where he
> wants to apply to college. We don't need to take much
> of your time; we'll be brief and to the point. Have you
> heard much about [the project]?

Find out what the person already knows so you are not
spending unnecessary time on these points. After making
your brief presentation, the most critical part of the conversation is to ask the prospective donor for the contribution.
Some people are better at this than others, but be sure to
ask. If you are uncomfortable with asking for money, be

sure to practice. Practice with people you know first to build your confidence.

There is an unwritten rule in fund-raising to ask for twice as much as you expect the donor to contribute. It may stun the prospective donor, but if done carefully it will not. The best way I have found to get around this is very graciously to add the word "hoping" to the request, as in "We were hoping you would be willing to contribute [amount] to the project." You want people to stretch their hearts and their pocketbooks.

This softens the request. Then comes the waiting. Let the contributor talk now. Silence can be the key to letting the contributor think through her or his response. The tendency is to interrupt the silence, as some conversationalists seem to think silence is deadly. Good closers know that silence is your friend.

Remember that the request is the most critical part of the appointment.

There are several common responses to asking for money. You should know how to answer each.

THE DELAY RESPONSE
"I need to talk to my spouse about this."
"Let me think about it."
"Can I get back to you on this?"

Delay responses are perhaps the most common. There are two ways to answer. One is simply to ask, "When would you like me to call you back on this?" The second method takes a little more moxie, so you need to be careful if you use it. This method is to push the prospective contributor a little by asking, "Is there a range that you were thinking about?" or "Are you thinking about a number you might be comfortable with?"

THE NEGATIVE RESPONSE

"No, that's much more then we can afford to give."

"I don't think we can help you at this time."

"Are you crazy? That's much more than I would consider contributing!"

Don't take any of these responses personally, whether they're positive or negative. Certainly it's better to have a positive response, but if you look at each of these negative responses there is a positive side to them. Your response to all of these could be "What number are you more comfortable with?"

Just as in the sales room, you must bring the solicitation to a close when romancing in the money room. You've asked for money, the prospect has hedged with his or her response, and now it's up to you to obtain the pledge by accommodating your request to the perceived limits. Set a specific dollar figure and address the concerns expressed. You might consider an offer to accept installment payments. Once you and the donor have agreed on an amount, present a donor card for his or her signature to finalize the commitment.

CHAPTER 9

The Classroom

The exchange of information is one of the most funda-mental elements of a good romance. Earnest young lovers describe themselves as "getting to know each other," while old married couples express the time-honored cliché "We know each other like the back of our hands." But whether new or old, successful romances are characterized by that *King and I* sense of "getting to know all about you" as part of an ongoing classroom of love.

Communicators, too, must learn the essential skills for transferring information and making their "classrooms" places where learning is made more memorable. Whether in an actual classroom, or at a business presentation or lecture, the informative presentation depends on engaging the listeners in order to be successful.

You cannot engage listeners or students with informa-tional presentations unless you motivate them to learn. Be-fore someone can truly learn, they need to be motivated to believe the information is interesting and important to them. You start with this task, of course, by expressing in-terest in the topic yourself. If the speaker seems bored and listless, the listening audience is sure to follow suit.

Each year, I give a four-hour course on federal court jurisdiction, with a particular emphasis on the intricacies of various federal preemption doctrines. Now, this lecture doesn't address a single question asked by Congress of potential nominees for the U.S. Supreme Court, nor of anyone else for that matter. To some, this subject is a real yawner. But not to me. I enthusiastically deliver my lecture on federal jurisdiction, comparing my love of these rules and corollaries to my affection for high school geometry. Learning this subject helps us all to understand how state and federal courts fit together in the jigsaw puzzle called our system of jurisprudence. My listeners might think I'm a bit of a nerd, but the enthusiasm can be contagious—they're paying attention and learning.

You must also combine your own enthusiasm with reasons why the listeners should be enthusiastic learners as well. As I'll show below, your task as an informational speaker or teacher is to prove to those in your "classroom" that listening and learning will provide them with benefits and allow them to avoid the pitfalls one can encounter from ignorance on the subject. And certainly you must, as we'll discuss, convince the listeners that they can learn this subject. If my college organic chemistry instructor had been more clear, perhaps I would have become a doctor, per the original plan.

As I discussed when addressing the romancing of other rooms, our effort to romance the classroom must first and foremost consider who is in that classroom trying to learn. We've used a multitude of phrases to capture this prerequisite: "listen while you talk," "keep your eye off the 'I'," and perhaps most essentially, use the ABC of communication: "audience before content." Thus, before we explore the techniques for communicating information in an engaging way, it is important to consider the varying ways in which people learn.

The Ways That People Learn

Educational authorities generally agree that each of us learns by using one or more of the following four methods: auditory, visual, experiential, or independent. Therefore, when we are romancing our classrooms, we must be aware that our listeners consist of each of these types of learners.

Auditory learners prefer to listen. They like the radio, talk shows, and music. Auditory learners are good at remembering lyrics and specific sounds. They learn more by varying sound dimensions through pitch, pace, and inserting music or sound effects. Try using ear candy: audiotapes, choral responses, discussion, debate, and dramatic readings.

Visual learners will opt to read books, newspapers, and magazines. They like to watch television, videos, and DVDs. Visual learners like to observe others work and perform, and learn more with visual aids, overhead projections, computer presentations, and flip charts. Try using eye candy: short video clips, filmstrips, laser disk images, films, slides, overhead transparencies, computer displays, and animations.

Experiential learners like to touch things and experience events. They are antsy, and often move their mouths, hands, and feet at the same time. They want to be totally involved. They love telling and listening to stories because you can experience the story in your imagination. They learn best by being involved in a project or group interaction. Try using hand candy: field trips, building projects, and role-playing.

Independent learners favor working alone, taking things apart and putting them back together. They learn quickly and like to be in charge of what they are being taught. Independent learners are very goal oriented and want to know how the material being learned can help them achieve their mission. They are better listeners one-on-one rather than in a group. They learn better if they are given the titles of secondary sources, and can go off and do a project by themselves after hearing about it in a group. Try using independent candy: assignments, research, library work, and independent projects.

For example, when we buy a new computer, each of us learns how to use it through our own style of learning. The auditory learner might call up the technical support hot line and ask for verbal directions. The visual learner, on the other hand, could navigate this initiation process through visual image tutorials, graphic illustrations, and accompanying video displays. The experiential learner simply turns on the computer and by "touch and feel" eventually becomes an expert. Finally, the independent learner may work his or her way through the owner's manual and buy a "how to" guide from the local bookstore.

For the speaker attempting to romance this multifaceted classroom, it is essential to combine techniques that will reach each of these various learners. We must be like William Shakespeare writing informational plays for our Globe Theatre–type classrooms, appealing simultaneously to people of varying backgrounds and styles.

Presenting Engaging and Memorable Information

When you are presenting information, you must do so in a way that engages all members of the audience. As a threshold matter, you must be certain that the information is understood and can be retained. Try watching a television station broadcasting in a language you do not speak.

You won't stay tuned for very long, and you most likely will remember absolutely nothing.

Regrettably, the same results occur in countless classroom and other settings when the presenters forget to communicate in an understandable and interesting manner. I will focus below on ways speakers can engage their audiences with information—both visually and otherwise—to make learning easier and more successful.

Simplify the Complex

A simple example shows how hard it is to communicate with words alone. Try to demonstrate how to tie a shoe. Imagine you can't use anything other than words: no hand gestures, no drawing on the boards, no pointing down at your shoes. Asking your audience to visualize one red and one yellow shoelace helps, but still the task is virtually impossible.

Now imagine that same speech with a visual aid. Maybe it's a large shoe, like the one that housed the little old lady with so many children, with two different colored laces. Now your audience can follow the sequence of tying a shoe much easier. If someone had never tied a shoe before it would be difficult to comprehend the instructions without the visual aid.

So we want to ask ourselves this question: How are we going to enhance the audience's ability to learn, since in our careers as communicators we will often be presenting complex information? For some of us, as soon as a graph goes up on the board we immediately tune out the speaker. Complex communication challenges are continuously upon us.

The first thing you're going to tell your audience is that it's not difficult to learn. Don't ever lead off your presentation with the statement that the information is extremely complex. It can be a self-fulfilling prophecy. Rather, you will want to break down the subject into its constituent parts, assuring the listeners at each stage that the information can be learned.

Let us suppose you had to talk about the human brain. You know the human brain is a complex organ. Maybe you're involved with a murder prosecution, where someone was hit over the head. You know that if you can't see the injury, and you're told the human brain is so complex that you'll never figure it out, then you will be baffled by a presentation on it. However, if you can see inside the brain you can actually visualize what you're learning and understand the part of the skull that is being discussed. If you can visualize what is being discussed, you think you can learn.

Some years ago, a student in my speech class at Stanford chose to teach us how to spot counterfeit money. We knew at the outset that this must be a challenge, or these criminals would not be able to pull off the monetary fraud with such ease—and right under the eyes of bankers at financial institutions. Rather than overwhelm us with complexity, my student put up enlarged images of counterfeit $20 bills right next to enlargements of the genuine article. He focused our attention in a riveting manner on the subtle graphic techniques employed by counterfeiters. A fascinating presentation, and one I've remembered in detail every time I examine Andrew Jackson's flowing locks on the twenty spots in my wallet.

If the audience thinks it cannot learn, it will not learn. Sometimes communicators emphasize how complex the information is because it builds them up, without realizing how this tears the audience down. You will be faced with that awful moment as a communicator when the audience is looking at you but not tracking. They're looking at you, but they'll never remember what you said. The self-centered presenters don't care, and are perfectly willing to leave their listeners behind. But great communicators of information don't leave them behind, because your job is to get them to learn.

Teach the Unknown in Terms of the Known

How do you get your listeners to learn? You must teach them the unknown in terms of the known. Define unknown terms. If you're giving a speech about a topic that someone knows nothing about, you must break the topic into its constituent parts.

During one of the presidential debates held in 1980, Ronald Reagan was asked to tell how many unemployed people there were in America. He said that if you lined up every person in this country who is unemployed at this time and put them three feet away from each other, that line of unemployed people would stretch from Los Angeles, California, to New York City. This was a great response because the abstract numeric figure was tied to a concrete image.

Motivate to Learn

A romance will not flourish if the person you are courting is not interested in learning more about you. You must share personal information demonstrating that you're intriguing and fascinating—not just in the abstract, but to that person in particular.

One of the critical aspects, therefore, of romancing the classroom is to convince the listeners that learning the proffered information will have particular meaning and significance for them. Motivating your listeners to learn might be as simple as setting forth why the information is valuable; for example, it may assist them in avoiding unpleasant consequences.

The age-old sales pitch that always motivates a buyer goes something like this: A young man earning his way through college knocks on a door. A woman anwers. The young man is selling portable vacuums. Why should she buy one? He throws dirt on the carpet, thus giving her a reason to buy the portable vacuum. She says, "Oh my God, there's dirt all over the carpet." His answer: "Don't you worry, because this vacuum works beautifully." This simple technique says to the prospective customer: "I'm going to motivate you to buy this portable vacuum."

Let me tell you about one student in my class a few years ago. He started a demonstration speech off by saying, "Can I ask all of you to raise your hand if you're under the age of twenty-one?" Three-fourths of the class members raised their hand. "Well, that's terrific," he said. "How many of you would like to leave tonight's class with a New Jersey driver's license that says you're twenty-three-years old?" The same hands shot up immediately. This student did his speech on how to make a New Jersey's driver's license. He had a big board he'd made into a New Jersey license, with all the fancy lettering. Cut out of the board was space for a person to fit his or her face in, like a carnival cutout. Using a Polaroid at the right distance, he took a photo of the board and the person's face. The Polaroid was the exact size of a New Jersey license. If I had not intervened, everyone would have left that night's session with a New Jersey driver's license that had a birth date that made them twenty-three years old. But during this speech my students were certainly motivated to learn.

Why did they listen to this information? The answer is because they could get something from it. Inspiring and motivating others to learn is key.

Be SMART

To give a strong, informative presentation, you've got to be SMART: simple, memorable, apt, reactive, and trustworthy.

Simple

You start with *simple*. Make your speech simple. Do this step by step. You're not going to tell your audience the subject is complex, and you're going to show that seeing is believing. For many years now, I've witnessed students fail in their attempts to demonstrate the art of origami—the Japanese technique for folding paper into beautiful shapes. The students begin by telling us we will each fold paper into the shape of a stork. However, there are so many folds, and the explanations are so intricate, that they cannot convey the information simply—or successfully—in a three-minute speech.

In contrast, you can teach people one element—the toss—of the seemingly complex task of juggling three balls. The speaker starts by telling the audience that juggling is as simple as tossing a lemon from one hand to the other. After demonstrating this easy step, the speaker introduces an orange into the mix, but tells the listeners to keep their eyes focused on the lemon in the two-object toss. Of course, the lemon still goes from one hand to the other as it did in the initial toss. Finally, the speaker takes the last step, adding one more orange to the now clear example of juggling. Again, however, the speaker admonishes the audience to stay focused on the lemon—easily contrasted in color to the other two objects. And again, the toss is the same, simply from hand to hand. You don't (and can't) teach the audience the complex task of juggling in three minutes, only the far simpler intermediate step of the straightforward toss of a lemon.

Memorable

The information you present has to be *memorable*. You know, seeing is believing, but more importantly, *seeing is remembering*. Use striking visual aids that reach out and grab the audience! Graphs and charts don't always accomplish this, but if you must use them, make sure they are bold and colorful.

Apt

The A in SMART stands for *apt*. Information has to be suitable to the situation, and an appropriate illustration for the point must be presented. In a recent speech class, one of my students made a heartfelt presentation about losing weight. He even shared with us that in one year he had gone from a forty-inch waist to a thirty-two-inch waist. However, he then presented information at a graduate school level on the complexities of food and body chemistry. The topic and the speaker's credibility were engaging. The supporting information was not suited to the audience and, therefore, not apt.

Reactive

Let's go to the R in SMART. You've got to be *reactive*. Listen while you talk. Are they following you? Simply put, you must adapt your information and visual aids to the needs of the audience, and react when listeners do not appear to be interested.

For example, several years ago I allowed a member of the local community to take my speech class for undergraduates. Although she was older than the students, it worked well until the night for her demonstration speech. She decided to make her presentation on how to lay out your backyard vegetable garden so as to maximize its productivity. Her speech was simple and well delivered, and her information was apt to her topic; however, to a class of twenty-five students living in dormitories, her information was not reactive to the audience at hand. Her topic simply didn't matter to her listeners, and their polite but disinterested reaction spoke volumes.

Trustworthy

The last letter in SMART is the T. That stands for *trustworthy*. Ultimately, information must be perceived as credible—both by way of source and presentation—in order to be effective. For example, I heard a student speak on the subject of self-defense for women. She said, without attribution, that in the United States, two out of three women will be sexually assaulted in their lifetimes. The statistic was not sourced and seemed exaggerated, unless the definition was so broad as to lack trustworthiness. In such a situation, the absence of a credible source for the incredible information substantially weakens the presentation.

By the same token, the presenter can put forth information in such a way that its trustworthiness can reasonably be questioned. Does the speaker seem to know what he or she is talking about? Is the presentation well supported with professional-looking visual aids and credible and expert evidence?

I tried a case many years ago that was every lawyer's nightmare. I put on an expert psychiatrist to testify as to the invalidity of the emotional distress damages being claimed by the other side. On cross-examination, the opposing lawyer asked my witness if he would agree that the quality of an expert's scholarship is directly related to the quality of the journals in which he or she publishes his or her research. Of course, he agreed. The lawyer then asked if, in contrast, a physician published in less than reputable publications, would that cause one to question the quality of the person's expertise. Again, and without hesitation, my witness agreed. The cross-examining lawyer then flipped open a recent edition of *Playboy* magazine and asked if it wasn't true that *this* witness had published his most recent article in that publication. When the witness was forced to agree, I felt compelled to ask for a bathroom break! Trustworthiness of information is often based on perception.

Bring Your Visual Aids to Life

In this section of the chapter we'll learn how to harness the power of visual aids—how to communicate information in more than just words. Almost any communication can be made clearer and more memorable and entertaining with the use of visual aids or props. Remember: appearance is key to making a good impression on a date—you've got to look sharp! When giving a presentation, the use of visual aids will excite your audience and help make your speech memorable.

Visual aids should be considered by *every* presenter in *every* speech situation. Studies on the subject show that the use of visual aids in a speech substantially increases an audience's comprehension of the information presented, as well as the audience's retention of that information days, weeks, and months later. This is not surprising, because it comports with our own experiences—understanding things more clearly when they are visually illustrated and remembering information and events better when we can store a visual picture or cue in our memories.

Visual aids can do so many different things for an audience. They can reveal; they can clarify; they can inspire; and they can motivate.

Let's try this one on. The speech was called "The Death of a Department." It was given at San Francisco State University, several years ago, by the chair of a department to an assembled room of faculty and students. Her thesis was that the department was going to die for lack of financing because of budget cuts. To illustrate that point, she could have told her audience how many classes were being cut, or even used a pie chart showing the budget numbers; instead, she used a visual aid showing the following year's course catalog with a dark line through every course that would be cut. It literally showed the death of a department. *The visual aid said it all.* So your visual aid can tell a story, and it can communicate ideas.

Rules for Bringing Your Visual Aids to Life

- **Follow the farthest person rule.** You locate the person who is farthest away from you in the room and then adjust your visual aid so that he or she can see it. Be sure to ask, "Can anybody not see this?" and if someone can't see it, you either enlarge it, drop it if you can't change it, or bring the person closer in.

- **Control the attention.** Tell the audience what you want it to pay attention to in the visual aid. Audiences will almost always do what you tell them to do, such as moving to different locations at your request. You are in charge of your presentation, and you're in charge of what you want the audience to pay attention to.

  There is an apocryphal story about a trial lawyer in the last century who concluded his closing argument to the jury, returned to counsel's table, and lit up a cigar while beginning to listen to his youthful opponent's rebuttal argument. As the opposing attorney continued, the jury seemed distracted. The ash on the first attorney's cigar just kept getting longer, and longer, and longer . . . but never dropped off. The jury, mesmerized by the hanging ash, could not pay attention to the young lawyer's arguments, and his client lost the case. Later, the wily older lawyer revealed his visual aid trick: the insertion of a metal rod into the cigar such that the ash would never fall off. That lawyer knew the principle of controlling attention with visual aids.

- **When you are done with the visual aid, put it away.** Get rid of it. If I give my speech and I leave a model of the human brain out on the desk while I talk, the listeners will be paying attention to that. The closer the visual aid is, the more they will focus on it. The more boring the speech, the more they'll look around for things to look at.

- **Be prepared for things to go wrong; they often do.** Speakers will tell you that the use of visual aids must be choreographed. Since such choreography can be unpredictable, you must always be prepared for the possibility that things can go wrong. For example, if you are using a stack of transparency slides on an overhead projector, number them so that if you accidentally drop them you can easily put them back in order, and thus avoid the delay and distraction caused by fumbling with them during the speech.

By the same token, I always come prepared with extra copies of a hard disk containing the computer-generated visual aids. My Boy Scout "always prepared" approach includes bringing an extension cord, a replacement bulb for the computer projector, and extra copies of any handouts. I try always to arrive early and check out the room and the arrangements, knowing exactly where the local copy shop is located in case last minute corrections are necessary.

In my class a couple of years ago, there was a demonstration speech on how you can win a $20 bet in a bar. My student brought in a hanger and a penny. He held the hanger upside down and put the penny on its spindle. Putting his finger through the hanger, he told us he was going to spin it around, and when he was done the penny would still be on the spindle. He delivered his entire speech on how he could win this bet. He reached the crescendo, and then put his finger into the hanger and spun it around. Well, the penny went flying! Did he say, "Oh my goodness, it didn't work"? No! He was ready for things to go wrong. His next words were "First do it this way, and then raise the bet to double or nothing." So he did it again, and that time he got it right. Most of us thought he had planned it. Later, we learned that his original demonstration hadn't gone as desired. You've got to not let them see you sweat.

- **Avoid the family slide show.** You do not want to say, "The next visual aid is . . . The next visual aid is . . ." This raises the problem with PowerPoint. PowerPoint is great tool. But it has a risk of being hypnotizing—as in mesmerizing, as in boring. The audience just sits and stares. My dad did a wonderful slide show, but he always said, "The next slide is . . . The next slide is . . ." Adopting the style of the family slide show is what you want to avoid in this particular setting.

- **Give your visual aid a verbal setting.** Every time you present a visual aid you should give it a verbal setting. This includes descriptive labels on charts, graphs, transparencies, slides, and computer-generated images. When you put forward your visual aid to the audience, you should tell the listeners what they are seeing and what its significance is to the information point you are making, and verbally place it in context in conjunction with the other visual aids used in the speech.

  During trials, I often use a computer-generated timeline to allow the judge or jury to follow graphically the events as I anticipate they will be supported to have occurred under the evidence. The timeline program I use looks like a long horizontal tube moving forward chronologically, with the points in time tied to the events under scrutiny in the case. The tube is colorful, and the verbal entries are limited and clearly printed.

  The temptation, however, is to let the visual aids give the speech for you. This is a mistake. You're the speaker, and the listeners expect you to present the information to them. As a general rule, I say that in speeches on complex topics, the audience's eyes should be on the speaker at least 50 percent of the time. In speeches on less intricate subjects, the audience should focus on the speaker at least 80 percent of the time allotted.

  And under no circumstances should you give a speech in the dark. You cancel one of the best tools in your romancing box: your eye contact with the audience. In addition, the temptation for the audience to sleep increases when the environment is just ripe for a short snooze!

- **Be aware of the impact of your visual aids.** They may look perfectly fine at home, but then they fall apart when you present them. One student a few years ago did a speech in my class on how to start a motorcycle. He rode it in through the door, past the audience, and up onto the stage, to the front of the audience. There was a table there, and he lifted the motorcycle on top of the table. Now this guy was impressive. Don't get discouraged if you're not that brave or strong!

VISUAL AIDS REVIEW QUESTIONS

1. What in your speech needs to be simplified? _____

   _____

2. How do you teach the unknown? _____

   _____

3. What are you motivating them to do? _____

   _____

4. What is the first thing you need to know? _____

   _____

5. What are you never going to tell a group again in your life? _____

   _____

6. If the audience thinks it cannot learn, it will not _____

   _____

7. Great communicators don't _____ audiences _____?

   _____

8. If you're giving a speech about a topic that someone knows nothing about, you've got to break it down into _____

   _____

9. Like Ronald Reagan, use _____.

   _____

10. Why should an audience listen to your information? _____

    _____

11. What method is used to present complex information? _____

    _____

12. Should you try to put as much information as possible in a visual aid? ___

    _____

13. What does SMART stand for? _____

    _____

14. Seeing is? _____
_____

15. Listen while you _____.
_____

16. You have to give visual aids _____ settings.
_____

17. What is the farthest person rule? _____
_____

18. What should you do with visual aids when you are done with them? ____
_____

19. Avoid the family _____ show.

ANSWERS TO VISUAL AIDS REVIEW QUESTIONS

1. Complex information.

2. You teach the unknown in terms of the known.

3. You are motivating them to learn.

4. Your audience.

5. That this is complicated.

6. It will not *learn*.

7. Don't *leave* audiences *behind*.

8. Its constituent parts.

9. A concrete image.

10. They're going to get something from it.

11. The step-by-step method. You need to take it apart and present it step-by-step.

12. No. Don't overload a visual aid; you only want to show the pertinent information.

13. SMART = simple, memorable, apt, reactive, trustworthy.

14. Seeing is *believing,* but seeing is also *remembering.*

15. Listen while you *talk.*

16. You have to give visual aids *verbal* settings.

17. Make sure your visual aid can be seen and read by the person farthest away. Ask your audience, "Who can't see this?"

18. Put all your visual aids away when you are done with them.

19. Avoid the family *slide* show.

VISUAL AIDS CHECKLIST

1. Follow the farthest person rule.

2. Be sure you control the audience's attention.

3. Be prepared—check your equipment, and have backups available.

4. Give your visual aids verbal settings.

5. Don't subject your audience to the family slide show.

CHAPTER 10

The Ballroom

When people think of someone addressing an audience, the first image that often comes to mind is a special occasion. For example, we think of a toast at a wedding, a presentation at an awards ceremony, or a graduation address. Maybe it is something as celebratory as a good-natured roast given upon a coworker's retirement.

Our thoughts turn to these examples because we have come to associate such occasions with the speeches that give them meaning and memory. In fact, the techniques for romancing a room are uniquely suited to the special-occasion setting where you must court the crowd in an actual or figurative "ballroom." In such settings, the speaker must romance the crowd with words and images that engage, and that are memorable and enhance long-term relationships.

Some of our country's most famous speeches have been given as part of special occasions: Lincoln's 1863 address dedicating the soldiers' cemetery at Gettysburg, Roosevelt's stirring 1941 speech to a joint session of Congress seeking a declaration of war, and John Kennedy's euphonic 1961 inaugural address. In fact, throughout the history of the world, stirring speeches have made special events remembered for the ages. One need only think of Socrates' address to his judges as he faced the fatal hemlock punishment, Mark Antony's fabled "Friends, Romans, Countrymen" eulogy over the body of Julius Caesar, Gandhi's spirited speech in self-defense against trumped-up charges of sedition, and King Edward's "the woman I love" speech in abdication of the English throne.

Special-occasion speeches are not limited in any way to presentations made by famous persons on historical events. Rather, anyone could be asked to make such presentations. The opportunities for giving such speeches are as varied as the types of celebrations and events we plan and attend throughout our lives: graduations, retirements, weddings, awards ceremonies, conventions, political events, testimonial dinners, holiday celebrations, and funerals.

A special-occasion speech is just that: a speech given to a group of people gathered together for a distinct purpose. When we are involved in a romantic relationship, we plan special days and moments, like the first dinner with the parents, a marriage proposal, or an anniversary dinner, with an eye toward making everything just right. We want to say and do the right things so as to make the moment special.

So, too, with special-occasion speaking. Special-occasion speaking is about *giving a speech in context*. We romance our listeners in these special "ballroom" settings by showing a heightened sensitivity to the demands and expectations of the particular situation. You need to understand clearly the distinguishing factors of a speech in context.

What we mean by a special-occasion speech, or a speech in context, is a speech in which you show a special sensitivity to the audience. You should be concerned about two principal things: *What is the occasion?* and *Who is the audi-*

ence? First, the occasion: What's the setting? What's the program? What's the purpose of this occasion? Is the occasion festive, solemn, celebratory, glib? For the *nature of the occasion* dictates the implicit communication rules for the moment. When George W. Bush delivered his speech to Congress about the terrorist attack on the World Trade Center, it was no time for glib communications. It was a somber and serious occasion. In contrast, when the president makes his annual address to the Gridiron Club in response to the ribbing given by the Washington press corps, the evening is lighthearted and certainly not the occasion for a dry discussion of economic policies.

Speakers who violate the implicit rules and expectations of such occasions will achieve the opposite of a good romance—they will turn off the audience and deflate the special occasion. Therefore, a speaker delivering a valedictorian address at a high school graduation operates under the implicit rule mandated by the situation: speak glowingly of the shared educational experience and of the institution that provided it. Thus, if a speaker uses the occasion as a platform to espouse his or her views on a controversial subject (e.g., abortion, capital punishment, etc.), the rules have been broken and the room has been unromanced!

These implicit communication rules can be broken quite by accident. A friend of mine went to a rehearsal dinner in preparation for the wedding of two of his close friends. The occasion called for breezy toasts filled with reverie for the upcoming event, as the members of the families, young and old, gathered for the celebratory dinner. My friend thought he was being funny when he regaled the audience with a story about a recent happening in the life of the bethrothed couple. However, the story arose in the context of their home, where they were living together—a fact not known and not appreciated by many of the older guests: the grandparents, the aunts and uncles, and the rest. The faux pas certainly did not help to romance this romance.

When you consider the occasion, you need to analyze the physical setting as well. Is the venue of the gathering formal or informal? What limits, if any, exist on the types of visual aids you can present (e.g., the availability of a screen for a large computer-generated presentation)? Will you be speaking with or without a microphone? These and other questions assist you in adapting your speech to the occasion itself.

Recently, for example, I was asked to be one of several presenters honoring my high school speech coach on the joint occasion of his twenty-fifth year of teaching and the fiftieth year of the speech program at my alma mater. I scoped out the room and determined that I could visually illustrate my presentation with slides. I went through the old yearbooks, snapped slides of the highlighted events, and was able to put on a "this is your life" presentation in the large ballroom. It sure beat the alternative of a dry, words-only speech.

As you examine the occasion, you will also want to look into the nature of the program in which you are participating. Where will you be speaking in the lineup of speakers? Will someone be introducing you? Will your speech be followed by questions and answers or other audience feedback? The answers to each of these questions will assist you in tailoring your presentation to the occasion planned by the persons or group who have asked you to speak.

Next, the audience: Who is in the audience, and what are the ties that bind it to this special moment? How large will the group be, and what will it have heard from others that day or at previous gatherings? What are the audience's expectations arising from this occasion? What is the group's attention span, particularly in light of what it has been told in advance as to the expected length of the presentation?

As in other romancing situations, you must gear your presentation to the audience before you. If, for example, you are addressing a Democratic fund-raiser, a reverential reference to Ronald Reagan might not be your first choice. Similarly, if you are giving an award to a movie director, it would not be the best time to expound your view that the movie industry is polluting the minds of our children.

One other thing to remember about special-occasion speaking, more than in any other setting, is that *you must be aware of the audience's attention span.* How long are you expected to speak? Find out, and by all means do not exceed the time limit.

As in a romance, you can ruin the special occasion if your timing is off. In special-occasion settings, the audience almost always has a sense (obtained from the program or the nature of the occasion) as to the length of the presentation. Thus, as is the case in most speeches, the watch is your most important tool.

There is something to be said of the fact that Edward Everett, the main speaker at the dedication of the Gettysburg cemetery, wrote President Lincoln some days later and said: "I shall be glad if I could flatter myself that I came as near to the central idea of the occasion in two hours as you did in two minutes." And, of course, Lincoln understood well the essence of an audience's time expectations when he graciously replied to Everett with these words: "In our respective parts yesterday, you could not have been excused to make a short address, nor I a long one."

As speakers ourselves on special occasions, we must always ask the planners of an event (and perhaps audience members in advance) of the expected length of the presentation. Far too often speakers fail to ask or adhere to the recommendation regarding this sensitive matter–leaving all of us to suffer as we have through the two-hour graduation speech, the forty-minute eulogy, or the ten-minute acceptance of an award. There's a reason they use the "red-light" system for the Academy Award acceptance speeches. If we want to romance our rooms, we must pay close attention to that light in our presentations.

Here are some brief pointers to remember when giving various special-occasion speeches.

Eulogies

Let's start with a basic special-occasion speech: a eulogy. What is a eulogy? It's a speech at a funeral that is a tribute to the deceased. What's the fundamental rule in giving a eulogy? *Do not speak ill of the dead.* You don't say when eulogizing someone, "Before I tell you about so-and-so's life, I'd like to tell you about a couple things he did to get himself into trouble." This violates the expectation.

Next, you acknowledge the fact of death. You ease the audience's realization of its own mortality. You move the audience from a relationship with the deceased in the present, to a relationship in the past. Then you fashion a way that the audience can deal with this new relationship.

There have been many famous eulogies. President Reagan gave, I think, one of the best eulogies ever for the seven people who died in the *Challenger* explosion. He started this famous eulogy by saying, "We come together today to mourn the loss of seven brave Americans. To share the grief that we all feel, and perhaps in that sharing, to find the strength to bear our sorrow, and the courage to look for the seeds of hope." Then he went on to talk about each of the seven people.

I've been teaching eulogies my whole career as a teacher

at Stanford, and until five years ago I had never given a single eulogy. Then I gave four in one year: for my father, my mother, my aunt, and my niece. This was hard, but now I have a true appreciation for effective, appropriate, and moving eulogies.

The eulogy is different than other kinds of special-occasion speeches in the sense that the audience or congregation may have very different needs that the speaker must address. Some in the gathering may simply want to grieve and to hear words that give way to the tears that must flow. Others may be harboring feelings of anger at the loss, perhaps because of its seeming senselessness. Still others look upon the event as a celebration of the deceased's life and want to hear uplifting and perhaps even lighthearted words. Finally, many of the people may be in attendance not because they knew the deceased, but out of support for those who have been left behind.

The trick for engaging this audience is to speak to and satisfy each of these needs in your eulogy. The effective eulogy will use words and images that do cause us to come face-to-face with the sadness of this loss. A story that shares the pain of the struggle that may have preceded death, an emotional aspect of the person's family, or the personal feeling of the speaker's own grief will allow the listeners to cry in unison with others. Certainly, the eulogy should describe the pain of loss, which also no doubt is one that will bind the group together.

And, perhaps surprisingly, an effective eulogy should be uplifting and even humorous, because it celebrates the deceased's life. In the eulogies I have delivered, I shared lighthearted stories about the deceased that were designed to illustrate one of their qualities that presumably many, if not most, of those in attendance had experienced themselves.

When I eulogized my father, a devoted weekend sailor, I

told the story of when he sent me out, full of encouragement, for my first race in a six-foot, single-sail El Toro. Even though I really wanted to be playing baseball, I went along. Amazingly, I was leading all other boats in this little in-harbor race around the first buoy, the second, and even the third. Then the sail on the little boat went flaccid, the other boats passed me one by one, and I ended up stuck in the marsh. My father *waded* over to me and, as I shared with the congregation, said six words I will never forget: "Maybe we better try Little League!" I did, and he never missed one of my baseball games for the next eight years.

Whether one shares an actual summary of the person's life or simply highlighted moments, the eulogist should share this information in a way that even those who did not know the deceased will come to understand. There is no higher praise for the speaker than for someone to say afterward, "I didn't even know him, but I really wished I had based on what you said." Job well done.

Like a good romance, the eulogy taps into the varied emotions of the listeners. Even in a short presentation, you can make them smile and cry. And if at all possible, try not to cry beyond control yourself. While understandable, the expression of such overwhelming emotion for too long a stretch imposes a burden on the listeners, rather than relieves them of their own.

The eulogy, like other special-occasion speeches, is an easy one in which to succeed. The listeners desperately want you to and will be remarkably supportive of any presentation, as long as it is thoughtful and prepared.

Welcome Speeches

When giving a welcome speech, think of yourself as the host. Ask yourself, What's the purpose of this meeting? Your goal is to generate goodwill. Almost always the mood will be cordial and happy. So what should you do? You identify the purpose of the occasion. You welcome the audience. Don't forget the entire point of the welcome speech! Who are you welcoming, and on whose behalf are you welcoming them? You also should identify guests of honor. If the president of the United States is in the audience, you identify him. Praise the sponsors. Build expectations, which means you need to know the program and to know where you're going. Many times the person giving the welcome speech must introduce the master of ceremonies. Once you finish your welcome speech, you should take a minute or two to do this. The organization of a good welcome speech is as follows:

- Identify the occasion and the purpose of the gathering
- Welcome the audience (i.e., who is welcomed, by whom, and why)
- Identify any guest or guests of honor
- Praise the sponsors
- Build expectations for the program or event
- Restate the welcome in closing and wish everyone success
- Introduce the master of ceremonies or the following speaker

Often, the welcome speaker is a member of the group that is sponsoring the event. If the audience is comprised solely of insiders, then inside references may and should be used. However, if the audience is more mixed, then the welcome speaker should resist the temptation to make remarks that leave a noticeable segment of the listeners going "Huh?"

My favorite welcome presentation is in the *Wizard of Oz*, when the mayor of Munchkin Land welcomes Dorothy Gale to this wonderful world and tries to make her feel right at home. The welcome speaker's job is just this simple.

Master of Ceremonies

The master of ceremonies is the person who makes the whole event flow. The master of ceremonies presides at the function, runs the show, and establishes the ongoing atmosphere for the event. While the emcee is the central figure, he or she does not play center stage.

Remember, there's only one rule for an emcee: *Don't screw up.* At the end of an evening, the audience won't say, "What a great emcee!" They should say, "What a great program." A good emcee introduces people, keeps the program going, and limits her or his remarks. If the emcee takes over too much, gets in the way, or tries to overdo it and becomes the focus of the evening, then he or she actually takes away from the event.

You know this from watching the Academy Awards. While Billy Crystal usually gave a nice opening introduction with a song-and-dance number, throughout the rest of the program he simply helped make transitions to different parts of the show. When David Letterman hosted one year, the program was criticized because Letterman tried to be the center of attention rather then place attention on the award winners and performers.

Great emcees make their job look easy. The program should be executed so smoothly you barely notice the emcee. Organization is everything. As the emcee, you are in charge of the way the event flows, because you're in charge of the pacing. You might try transition cards to keep track of timing.

When you are serving as the master of ceremonies, you should get up after being introduced and say something for about thirty seconds to establish a rapport with the audience. That first interaction with the audience is very important. Take it seriously, but don't take yourself seriously. If something goes wrong, you've got to deal with it. If a speaker's not there yet, you've got to adapt.

The emcee's main task is to manage the transitions, getting from one speaker to another. However, the emcee should not introduce people proposing toasts. The toast is the one speech where the speaker does not come to the podium. The emcee is still in charge of the toast, though, because the person giving the toast cannot start until he or she has made eye contact with the emcee. Great emcees must listen, be courteous, and use good taste. Just watch Oprah Winfrey move her show along and you've seen a master at work.

The trick for an effective emcee is to romance the room through the transitions from speaker to speaker. This requires that the speaker have plans for filling time when the schedule goes awry and tell stories that bind the people in the audience to themselves and the speakers.

You also must be prepared to deal with the occasional heckler or overactive audience participant. Never, I mean *never*, engage the heckler in a dialogue of disparagement (e.g., "Does your mother know you're out this late?"). Rather, you should skillfully and sometimes humorously deflect attention away from the heckling and back to the program. Almost always, the audience will be with you in this effort. If, of course, the heckler, whether sauced by alcohol or not, becomes disruptive, you'll need help from the program's sponsors or building security. Always know where and how to make this contact *before* you start your emcee gig.

The most important task as an emcee of a speaking program is to "open" and "close" the podium. In other words, when you go to the podium to begin the evening or after a break in the program (e.g., after a meal has been served), you open it by getting the audience's attention. This is not always an easy task if the attendees are engaged in animated conversations or if they are still eating. Be loud enough and direct their attention to the podium. When one part of the program is concluded, you close the podium. This means that you actually tell the audience there will be no further speeches at the time. Give people a direction to facilitate the podium's close (e.g., "Please enjoy your meal"). Otherwise, the audience will continue to stare at the podium, waiting for something else to happen.

The bottom line for the emcee is to make it look easy. It's like Joe DiMaggio when he played center field for the New York Yankees. He made the tough plays look easy because he was so well positioned and prepared when the ball left the bat.

Invocations or Benedictions

An invocation or benediction is a speech of reflection. It is time to pause for a moment before getting on with the speeches. The invocation speech should be nonsectarian and nondoctrinaire, meaning that as a speaker you must remember that people from a great variety of backgrounds are in the audience. Don't assume homogenous religion in an audience unless you know for a fact everyone in the audience shares the same religion. Do not dwell on religious symbols. Pick a one-point topic of reflection. Appeal to universal points: strength, guidance, generosity, and so on.

For example, a speaker could appeal to the nonsectarian, but appropriate, topic of "silence" for reflection. You could say that the program will be filled with words and the sounds of conversation, and you want everyone to pause and reflect on the value of silence. This topic, particularly if addressed by a layperson, would be appropriate for reflection and even illustrated by a dedicated moment of the topic itself.

Introductions

You will probably do this type of speech many times in your life. What makes a good introduction? A great introduction speech has three goals. The first goal is to build ethos for the person you are introducing. Build their credibility. You need to tell the audience why it should pay attention to or think highly of this speaker. The next thing you want to do is to build anticipation for the speech people are about to hear. Third, you build rapport, connect the audience to that person. Build a relationship between them. Provide a trait that the audience will admire. The absolute goal is for the audience to say, "I can't wait to hear this speech" or "I can't wait to meet this person." Remember: ethos, anticipation, rapport. Your purpose is to help the audience realize the worth of the person you're introducing. Give examples and instances of how that person demonstrates his or her qualities in action, making reference to a personal interaction with that speaker if you've had one. Show how remarkable his or her achievements are in the face of obstacles. Then summarize why that person has been chosen to speak.

SOME PRACTICAL TIPS

Be sure you pronounce the next speaker's name correctly. If he or she has to correct your pronunciation, it ruins your sense of credibility and connection to the audience. Get the speaker to spell it phonetically for you in a note if it is different.

Next, identify the speaker. Give your audience necessary information about the speaker, such as his or her background, connection to the group, and qualifications. Also, if it's a long speech, provide the title of the talk.

Follow the 10 percent rule; that is, your introduction should never be longer then 10 percent of the speech to follow. Adhere to this rule religiously. Never give an introduction longer than the speech you're introducing. You know, the Gettysburg address was 272 words. You can be short *and* effective.

Avoid clichés in your introductions, such as "Without further ado . . ." Repeat the speaker's name at the end. Follow through by saying the name at the beginning and at the end. Remain at the podium until the speaker arrives, shake his or her hand, and return to your seat.

Entertainment Speeches

Many times, speakers are asked to give speeches whose principal purpose is to entertain the audience. You are asking the listeners, as the drama texts tell us, to suspend their disbelief. In other words, the speech is not necessarily taken literally, particularly if its driving purpose is humor.

The success of a romantic relationship requires many moments that are lighthearted and fun. The entertainment speech is one in which you get to court the crowd for the fun of it. These speeches are given as part of after-dinner programs and at other events when the point of the gathering—or at least that part of the gathering—is to have fun.

Ordinarily, such presentations are one-point speeches. You pick a humorous topic, develop a lighthearted theme, and go with it. For example, my speech class's "final examination" takes place at a local restaurant where the students deliver special-occasion speeches (roasts, toasts, entertainment speeches) to their classmates and their invited guests. I always tell them three things: (1) it will be the most enjoyable final exam of their academic careers, (2) no rhyming speeches are allowed unless you are actually a good poet, and (3) the honor code is in place! This gets the tongue-in-cheek evening off to a good start.

Students address a wide variety of subjects with their entertainment speeches. I tell them that the topic must have some seeming relevance to the particular group (in this case college students). One year, a student gave his one-point speech about "inventions we wished we'd seen." He then talked about various absurd inventions (e.g., the "self-lighting cigarette") that could make them all lots of money after graduation. Another student gave a humorous "testimonial" called "The Lectern, Our Friend." The speech topic, ideal for a speech class audience, sang the praises of this essential piece of public-speaking furniture ("a friend upon whom we could always lean").

When you deliver a speech of entertainment, it must essentially be memorized or delivered with full eye contact at almost all times. The point of the speech requires direct contact with the audience. If you read such a speech, you lose your ability to spin the audience's sense of humor.

You also will often romance the room with entertainment by telling stories that illustrate your point. For example, one of my students once gave a speech to entertain on the power of rehearsal as a tool for public speakers. He told this story:

> The greatest speaker of our time, Sir Winston Churchill, used the power of rehearsal as he practiced the speeches that saved a nation during World War II. In fact, he rehearsed his speeches at every opportunity. One morning, when Sir Winston was in his tub, his valet heard his voice above the splashing. He opened the

door and asked, "Were you speaking to me, sir?" "No," replied
Churchill, annoyed at the interruption, "I'm addressing the House
of Commons."

When a speaker uses a story to illustrate a one-point entertainment speech, as here, the story must be pegged to
that point in a credible and clear way. If the story is a non
sequitur, the audience can feel let down. This is true even if
the illustrative story fits the profile of a joke. Even jokes
must fit the point being made.

If you're going to tell a joke, you must know the joke and
the punch line. There's nothing worse than flubbing a joke
halfway through it. And never start off a joke by saying,
"This is the funniest joke I've ever heard." It will never live
up to your listeners' expectations. If possible, personalize
the joke by referring to someone in the audience that you
know. Check with that person first to see if he or she is
okay with being mentioned.

Be sure to throw the punch line out clearly so that the
audience gets it, so that they truly follow the joke. *Stop the
joke when you're finished;* do not just keep prowling on after
the joke. Do not laugh all the way through the joke. Do not
omit important details, only to fill them in later, saying,
"Oh, I forgot to tell you this . . . "

Toasts

The toast is one of my favorite speeches. It has a wonderful history. It arose during Shakespeare's time. Apparently,
toast was placed at the bottom of a cup to add flavor and
improve the taste. Its purpose was to clarify the wines and
filter out sediment. The drink therefore became a "toast."

A toast is a brief speech of tribute to a person, an organization, or an idea. It should last sixty to ninety seconds, at

most. Typically a toast is clever, humorous, creative, insightful, eloquent, and maybe more.

A toast is an easy speech to give. Since you're not at a podium, you've got to be loud enough to get the attention of the audience. First of all, make eye contact with the master of ceremonies; otherwise, the program will not flow. Then raise your glass and say loudly, "I'd like to propose a toast . . ." Now you must decide whether to put the glass down or make a gesture. If you put the glass down to gesture, you have to pick it back up at the end. Also, there must be something in the glass. You simply don't give a toast when there's nothing in the glass. At the end of the toast, you hold up your glass and say, "Therefore, I propose a toast to so-and-so."

If the person you are toasting is present in the room, then everyone picks up a glass, gestures to where he or she is, and says, "Here, here." If, on the other hand, the person is not present in the room, then everyone is to repeat the closing words of the toast (e.g., "To the president of the United States").

The toast, like other occasional speeches, must be appropriate to the moment. In my speech class over the years, I have heard many toasts to people or ideas of common interest to a group of public-speaking students. One student, for example, toasted to "the hidden voice in the back of our heads." She said that all speech students, like her, had a hidden voice in the back of their heads that was talking to them as they gave their speeches (saying, for example, "Slow down," "You're screwing up," "They don't like you"). She toasted this voice and said that she wished for all the students that the voice would have very little to say. She expressed her wish that "our visual aids never melt" and that none of the students "ever ask for questions from a group of lawyers."

The toasts I have heard over the years have been clever and insightful. Students have given toasts to brevity, to our parent's children, to Mort (of Bazooka comics fame), to baseball, to hedonism, and, one of my favorites, to Ronald Reagan's barber, the "pompadour of power." Your choice of toast should be directed at romancing your room as well.

Roasts

How about giving a roast? A roast is a reverse testimonial. There is one key thing to understand about roasts. Roasts must be in good fun. *You cannot roast someone and have it be a genuine attack.* It's teasing. A roast is a speech that entertains, because you're asking the audience to suspend its belief about the person being roasted.

A roast, like other speeches to entertain, is usually a one-point speech. You fasten upon the subject's foible and then, through exaggeration, present it to the audience. For example, if you were roasting someone and wanted to tease him about being low-key, you might use lines like those that follow:

- He has the charisma of a speed bump.
- He's so boring, nobody goes looking for him in a game of hide-and-seek.
- As Churchill said of Clement Atlee, "He is a modest man . . . but then he has much to be modest about."

The comments are in the form of good-natured ribbing. To emphasize that the speech is given in good fun, always go to the person you are roasting (who absolutely must be in the room) and shake his or her hand. The meaning of that symbolic gesture is clear.

Presenting and Accepting Awards

One of the most common forms of the special-occasion speech involves the presentation and acceptance of awards. In our culture, we are fascinated with the ceremonies in which awards are bestowed. We have the Academy Awards, the Tonys, the Emmys, the People's Choice Awards, the MTV Video Music Awards, the Grammys, and many more. And they almost universally get high ratings. If only the award presenters and recipients remembered to romance the room during their remarks and speeches.

Presenting an award is a real art and usually is accompanied by the bestowal of a gift or other honor. The organization for such a speech is straightforward:

- State why the presentation is being made.
- Identify the recipient and explain why he or she is receiving the award.
- Explain why and how the person was selected for the honor.
- Identify the speaker's own satisfaction in presenting the award.
- Describe the gift/honor/award and indicate why it was chosen.
- Welcome the recipient to the stage and present the award.

Accepting an award requires a similar romancing skill, usually characterized by humility and gratitude. The outline for this speech is as follows:

- Express appreciation (briefly).
- Praise the person or organization that bestowed the award.
- Give credit for the achievement to others (but not too many!).
- Tell how the award is meaningful and will encourage you and others to further action and achievement.

In romance, it's called giving the other person "strokes." You cannot have a successful relationship without them. The same is true for a large number of special occasions.

The Day of the Speech

What do you do the day of the speech? Here is a check-list. On the day of the special-occasion speech, stand at the podium before the audience arrives. Sit at various places around the room to know what it's like. How does the stage look? Do the visual aids work? Check the mike before the audience arrives. And if you're giving a long speech, room temperature is very important, because you want the audience to be comfortable so that it will pay attention.

Don't call your office in the hour before the speech. It will distract you. Turn off your pager. You're on from the time you walk into the building. If you are the speaker, the audience is observing you, evaluating you, right from the start. Speak with the person introducing you. If you are making an introduction, speak with the person you're introducing. Bottom line: make it work; be creative.

Following the review of this chapter, on pages 126 through 130, are three examples of special-occasion speeches. The first is a roast, the second is a testimonial, and the third is a eulogy.

SPECIAL-OCCASION SPEECH REVIEW QUESTIONS

1. What is a speech in context? _____

2. What is the most important rule in giving a eulogy? _____
   _____

3. What are the characteristics of a good welcome speech? _____
   _____

4. What is the first rule of being the master of ceremonies? _____
   _____

5. What is the emcee in charge of? _____
   _____
   _____

6. What must you not assume when giving the invocation? _____
   _____

7. What is the winning checklist for making an introduction?
   a. _____
   b. _____
   c. _____
   d. _____

8. What should you *not* do when telling a joke? _____
   _____
   _____

9. What *should* you do when telling a joke? _____
   _____

10. What should you do when giving a toast? _____
    _____

11. Should you genuinely attack someone during a roast? _____
    _____

12. What are the six elements of giving an award? _____
    a. _____
    b. _____
    c. _____

d. _____

e. _____

f. _____

ANSWERS TO SPECIAL-OCCASION SPEECH REVIEW QUESTIONS

1. A special-occasion speech in which you show special sensitivity to the audience.

2. The most important rule of a eulogy is that you do not speak ill of the dead.

3. A welcome speech should be cordial, happy, and short. It should identify the guest of honor. It should praise the sponsors and build expectations.

4. The first rule of being the master of cermemonies is to not screw up.

5. The emcee is in charge of pacing, dealing with problems, transitions, rapport, filling time (if necessary), and opening and closing the podium.

6. When giving an invocation, one must *not* assume homogenous religion in the audience unless you know that for a fact.

7. The winning checklist for making an introduction is:

   a. Pronounce the speaker's name correctly.

   b. Give necessary information about the speaker: background, connection to the audience, qualifications, title of speech, and subject of the speech.

   c. Keep it short, at most 10 percent of the total speech.

   d. Repeat the name at the end.

8. When telling a joke, you should *not:* screw it up in the middle; start by saying, "This is a really funny joke"; laugh throughout the joke or omit key details; and try to come back and explain the details at the wrong time.

9. When telling a joke, you *should:* know the punch line, personalize the joke if possible, throw the punch line out clearly, test the joke on a friend, and stop when the joke is finished.

10. When giving a toast, you should stand at your seat and say, "I would like to propose a toast to [name the person]." When you are finished with the toast, you should raise your glass and say, "Here, here!"

11. No, when giving a roast you should never genuinely attack the person.

12. The six elements of giving an award are:

    a. State why the presentation is being made.

    b. Identify the recipient and explain why he or she is receiving the award.

    c. Explain why and how the person was selected for the honor.

    d. Identify the speaker's own satisfaction in presenting the award.

    e. Describe the gift/honor/award and indicate why it was chosen.

    f. Welcome the recipient to the stage and present the award.

CHECKLIST FOR THE DAY OF THE SPECIAL-OCCASION SPEECH

1. Stand at the podium before the audience arrives.

2. Know the room; sit at various places to know what is it like.

3. Check that the visual aids work from all parts of the room.

4. Check the mike.

5. Check the room temperature.

6. Don't call your office!

7. Turn off your pager or cell phone.

8. Be "on" from the time you walk into the building.

9. Speak with the person introducing you.

10. Or speak with the person you are introducing.

Bottom line: Make it work; be creative.

Roast of Yours Truly, Jim Wagstaffe

Final Examination Dinner
Stanford University
Class: Practical Speech Communication
By Craig Seipel

Jimmy Wagstaffe . . . what can I say about the man who regards free speech not as a right, but a continuous obligation?

During the past four months, for each speech we gave, Jim appeared to observe our progress patiently. But, my fellow orators, don't kid yourselves, let's be perfectly clear here! Jim would not even listen to our speeches if he didn't know that he was going to be speaking next!

While Jim never hesitated to point out the flaws in your speeches, he said the only trouble with his speaking was that he didn't know what to do with his hands. Well, Jim, did you ever consider covering your mouth with them?

In class, we wondered if Jim would ever stop talking? It's doubtful. . . . It didn't take us long to see that Jim Wagstaffe could get in the last word with an echo.

On a more serious note regarding Jimmy, we are all grateful for the improvement in our oratorical skills. . . . Jim, we all realize that although you may have continually blown your horn the loudest in class, it's only because you were in the biggest fog.

We recognize that although at this banquet you've been loud-mouthed, egotistical, and obnoxious, there's still something about you that continues to repel us all.

I roast you tonight, Jim. Thanks for everything. You are truly a person who is going places . . . the sooner, the better!

Testimonial

"Portrait of a Heavenly Boss"
In Tribute to Judge Spencer Williams
November 9, 2000
By James M. Wagstaffe

I am honored to be here and participate in this wonderful tribute and the unveiling of this marvelous portrait. I am here because of that aspect of my résumé of which I am most proud:

"1980–1982: Law Clerk to the Honorable Spencer Williams."

And what a learning fellowship!

It was twenty years ago, almost to the day, in a courtroom downstairs. Judge Williams said that I could come and watch the trial in progress since it had reached the closing argument stage. He told me, however, that one of the attorneys, while effective, was a bit of a blowhard. So I went in and watched from the peanut gallery. Now as I tell this story, you also have to realize that Bill Johnston, the judge's court reporter, is a character. The blowhard barrister got to the critical part of his argument and announced, "Ladies and gentlemen, nothing could be more crystal clear!" Bill Johnston chuckled, looked up from his transcription keys, and said, "Counsel, I didn't get that."

But Judge Williams always got it.

And he did so because he knew the wisdom of the advice shared with me on my very first day on the job: "Don't miss the big picture!"

As we prepare to unveil this portrait, I am reminded of how Judge Williams always kept his eye on the larger picture.

He told us as law clerks that, like the poet says, you chart your course not by the lights of passing ships . . . , but by the stars.

In fact, Judge Williams always navigated his life with celestial perspective. He played basketball at UCLA with Jackie Robinson; he saw active duty during World War II for the navy in the Pacific; he took contracts at Boalt from Professor David Snodgrass; he was secretary of human relations in Ronald Reagan's California cabinet.

Judge Williams was a district judge for almost thirty years. He authored more than three hundred published opinions. Many of them were covered on top of the newspaper's fold. They were courageous and far-seeing opinions, certifying nationwide class actions to protect consumers and preventing governmental regulators from acting improperly in closing financial institutions. The kinds of decisions that led to portraits hanging in federal courthouses.

My personal image of Judge Williams is an even more touching portrait of the man. Four years ago at my father's funeral, as I was grieving with my family, I looked out in the congregation, and there was Judge Williams. No one asked him to come, and he hardly knew my father. But he was there for me. . . .

Judge Williams has had an enduring commitment to preserve judicial independence. Concern that stagnation of the judicial compensation would adversely affect the federal judiciary's ability to attract highly qualified men and women led him to file *Adkins v. United States* to protect judicial salaries. And, twenty-three years ago, Judge Williams formed the Federal Judges Association and became its first president.

So, as we honor Judge Williams, I am reminded of the words Thomas Jefferson wrote to a friend in his later life: "I am an old man, but a very young gardener."

Judge Williams, you are a very young gardener. Indeed, and those of us here, particularly your present and past law clerks, are so proud to be the fruits of your garden.

A Verbal Album
Eulogy of Jean F. Wagstaffe
January 20, 1997
By James M. Wagstaffe

> The hands of our mother . . .
> The hands of a friend.
> Memories are deathless, binding us with mighty cables . . .

Swedish . . . practical . . . a file for every recipe, occasion, and expense . . . cross-indexed by source and date.

No nonsense here: not into image, networking, or self-help strategies.

But always willing to *lend a hand,* to support even when not touching:

1961: My first day of kindergarten. The long walk from 4 Robert S. Drive to Hillview School . . . with Mom . . . holding my five-year-old hand to show the way. But with a maternal caveat: "James, you're on your own the rest of the year!" A mother is not a person to lean on, but a person to make leaning unnecessary. . . .

Can you touch someone without your hands? . . . With your heart and with your love?

In a household of basketballs, baseball cards, and boys, Mom exposed her children (against all odds) to things of beauty and art: Saturday mornings listening to classical music on the hi-fi; fine china and manners on special occasions; and an ever-present love of the piano . . . skipping a generation before she could teach a grandson to play the "Moonlight Sonata."

A love of song is simply a caress set to music.

Finally, the daughters-in-law came. *Now* there was touching and hugging and sharing . . . cups of coffee on chilly mornings and lunches just to talk. Mom lended a sympathetic, knowing ear, showing these wives that the boys don't talk much about their feelings: you must listen not with the ears, but with the heart.

Foremost, my mother was a wife. Odd, these two: formal yet immensely compatible. To the eyes of a child, there was only one "quarrel" in forty-seven years of marriage for my mom and dad:

A summer day and Dad decided it was time to clean the gutters on the third floor. Typical of my dad, he used a jerry-rigged twenty-foot bamboo pole with a trowel strung at an angle—a Rube Goldberg contraption, like a long arm with a scooper hand. My mom stretched to guide the "hand" movements from an upstairs window. We kids were watching, with our grandfather watching us. Then Mom leaned out the window and began to crawl out on the ledge! Dad yelled at her with vigor and vim! "With love," my grandfather later reassured us.

Theirs was a love-filled marriage. Six children made miraculously from scratch. Their relationship was not gushingly affectionate . . . yet full of deep love and respect.

These snapshots capturing a lifetime. March, last year . . . children all around. My dad is sitting at the kitchen table, struggling to swallow Mom's soup, made with love. His hair thinning, almost gone—from the radiation. She touched, stroked, and then caressed what was left of his hair . . . saying, "Oh, Papa. Oh, Papa."

Then it was last Thursday night. We were there again . . . too soon. The doctor said it would be only hours. My sister-in-law was there, nearing the end of her ongoing vigil, holding Mom's hand. Mom was in bed, surrounded by her children.

Moistened eyes watched, waiting for each breath. She made no sound for hours, her eyes closed. Suddenly, at 7:00 P.M., her eyes opened, as wide as fifty-cent pieces. She spoke clearly and said: "I'm amazed!"

Sue asked: "Do you see something?"

"Yes."

Another asked: "Is it something we see?"

"No."

She was being touched herself by the hand of God. The bamboo stick from Dad . . . his hand, saying it was okay.

The hands of our mother . . . the hands of a friend—joined, reassuring us with the last sentence of her life: "I'm amazed!"

CHAPTER 11

The Story Room

"Tell me a story" is the cry of every young child before going to sleep at night. It is also the cry of every audience before it "goes to sleep," etherized by yet another speaker droning on without anecdotes or examples.

Anyone who doubts the compelling need for illustrative stories has never endured a typical family slide show presentation. The speaker clicks slide after slide showing scenery and landmarks, repeating the wearisome narrative: "The next slide is . . ." Without underlying stories, the family vacation is sterile and humdrum. In contrast, the electrifying speaker romances the audience with the stories behind the slides–the real stories to remember.

Most people think they aren't very good at telling stories. Nothing could be further from the truth. There is a powerful storyteller in all of us, and as I will show in this chapter, great storytelling is as easy as reciting the alphabet.

The Value of Storytelling

Novelist and Catholic priest Andrew Greeley tells us that to be told a story is a "primal, almost religious need." Stories allow us to simplify a complicated world and to express complex values with simple themes. It is in myths, fables, and allegories that we attempt to make sense of the difficult issues of life, death, triumph, and tragedy. Our religions, by way of example, serve to fill these needs, providing story-based explanations for the mysteries of life.

As you know, both my parents recently passed away. When I had to tell my young children their grandparents had died, it was made so much easier by being able to share with them the "story" of heaven, enhanced by the image that Grampa and Gramma were still alive in a different world. We share such complex ideas through simple stories because it is the way we can make sense of the mysteries of our existence.

It is through our stories that we are able to pass on such accumulated and lasting wisdom. The great storytellers used them to make points—Aesop's fables, Jesus' parables, Swift's allegories. Each brings with them large meaning within the simplicity of a story.

So much of communicating is striving for shared imaginings through stories. You want your listeners to see the images in their mind's eye and to be romanced by a compelling and engaging story.

As a trial lawyer, I have learned that storytelling is essential. The jury has to follow your story and reexperience the events (with any luck through your client's perspective!). And it all boils down to telling the jury a story that is easy to follow, engages the imagination, and illustrates your point.

It is no accident that lawyers often tell trial stories through communicators called "witnesses." If *your* witness is engaging and memorable, you will win *every time* as you use stories to romance your room. Otherwise, our trials and communications are just words.

For example, when a lawyer represents a person paralyzed in an accident, he could describe the injury using clinical terminology and technical language. However, the case would never become real or allow the jurors to feel the client's pain. It is much more effective to tell the jury a *story* about the client's daily life. A lawyer shows the jurors the day-to-day suffering of the person–the difficult and often impossible simple tasks such as eating and bathing. Counsel presents a "day-in-the-life" video that permits the client's suffering and indignities to be visualized and experienced by the jury. The treating doctor's clinical language is transformed into a memorable reality for each of the jurors.

A story can convey messages and meaning like no other communication tool. You can enliven your family gathering, your training session, or your job interview with a story that both illustrates your point and engages your listener as well.

Often when addressing groups, I want to illustrate the concept that "plain speaking" is a value and that there is much to be said for getting to the point. Here's one of the stories I use to communicate this theme.

Bruce Bean, a friend with whom I've worked for years, convinced me to attend an all-day seminar in Bakersfield titled "The Value of a Kind Word!" (The exclamation point showed they were really serious about civil discourse.) We traveled the few hours to the program and afterward decided to spend the night. The next morning, we drove home, stopping for breakfast at an off-road diner—you know, the kind where you park between the big rigs and ready yourself for high-octane coffee. Almost immediately after being seated at the chipped, red-topped Formica table, our waitress approached. She was an Alice B. Toklas look-alike, who no doubt had been working at this truck stop since the Huns took Rome. After we sat down, she rasped in a loud whiskey voice to no one in particular, "What'll ya have?" I ordered, and then it was Bruce's turn. (Now you have to understand Bruce—he can have a very pixieish sense of humor.) He said in his sweetest voice, "I'd like a cup of coffee, some scrambled eggs and . . . a kind word." Our Ms. Toklas rolled her eyes, grunted an acknowledgment, and harrumphed off to the kitchen. About ten minutes later, she returned, and after serving me, rattled Bruce's cup of coffee at him, and tossed his plate of scrambled eggs like it was a Frisbee. Then Bruce looked up at her and asked demurely, "How about that kind word?" The waitress responded without hesitation: "If I were you, I wouldn't eat them eggs!"

There's so much to this fabled story. By the time I finish, the listeners should feel like that old CBS television show *You Are There!* They can see the grizzled waitress, visualize Bruce's demeanor, and imagine the truck stop—all with reference to their own memory of analogous experiences. The story makes my point and brings variety to the presentation. Trust me, the audience wants more, not fewer, stories.

In the movie *City Slickers,* Billy Crystal and his friends from the big city face a crisis of ennui. Needing to rediscover the adventure of life, they decide to go on a cattle drive out west. At one point on the ride, Bruno Kirby, playing one of Crystal's cohorts, laments the breakdown in the relationship with his now-deceased father. Then he adds wistfully that even in the worst of times, they "could always talk about baseball." They could unite in their love of the national pastime, swapping stories about their shared experiences at the ballpark.

Stories in families provide the kind of continuity and meaning that solidify and restore bonds that can become weakened in this modern, fast-paced age. A family story, passed on from generation to generation, can communicate values of courage, strength, and love more than any lecture or punishment. Dr. Jerome Kagan, Ph.D., a professor of psychology at Harvard University, reminds us: "When kids hear family stories in which a family member has done something especially good or courageous, they conclude that there must be something good and powerful about themselves as well."

Storytelling was the medium through which people learned history, resolved disputes, and came to make sense of the phenomenon of the world around them. History comes alive and is maintained when told through stories. While you may know many details about George Washington, your image is of him standing in the boat crossing the Delaware. Back in 1860, Abraham Lincoln was elected president by repeating the yarn about his exploits as a rail-splitter. John F. Kennedy first received public notice as the hero of the *PT-109* war story. Such stories, far more than memorized facts and chronology, bring history to life. For example, if you ask most schoolchildren (or adults for that matter) to relate any single historical fact about Benjamin Franklin, they could recite very little. However, no one graduates from elementary school without learning the inspired story of Franklin "discovering" electricity by flying a kite during an electric storm. It is the story that remains fixed in our mind.

Today, as technology permits us to exchange messages instantaneously across the globe, it is ironic that our willingness to tell stories (and to learn how to tell stories) seems to be dwindling. We have all the tools to save time and communicate instantly, yet we feel rushed in all we do. As previously described in chapter 3, we live in an attention deficit world. The average attention span of an adult is seven minutes.

We are a society of channel surfers. When we go online,

we impatiently tap our finger on the keyboard if the log-in and modem connection takes longer than ten seconds. We don't have time to send a letter by mail—send it by fax! Even FedEx, which has made a successful industry model of overnight delivery, seems painfully slow to us if we need it to get there now.

Time for a story? Give it to me in a headline because that is all I can take right now. It's CliffsNotes, man! A book's too long. *The Jim Lehrer NewsHour* may get the geriatric viewers, but today's news junkies would rather watch *CNN Headline News* or, God forbid, "pop-up" news stories on MTV.

Allowing us to communicate instantly may have stripped us of what we need most from communications: shared imaginings and shared stories. In the advent of satellites and DIRECTV, there is very little chance you and I watched the same TV program last night. Frank McCourt, author of the Pulitzer Prize–winning memoir *Angela's Ashes,* observes that there is little time set aside in our culture for children to listen to stories: "I think TV is destroying story-telling." He adds, "My mother used to turn out the lights to save the candles, and we sat around talking, looking at the coals in the grate, and the talk and the ghost stories would make the nights better than anything I have seen on Broadway."

There is a cure to our schizophrenic need for stories and the lack of time to tell them. As speakers and communicators, we must relearn the art of storytelling because a good story expands our attention spans. Director Steven Spielberg knows this very well, as time after time he brings millions of people back to the theater with old-fashioned good stories. We must learn the same lesson.

The Art of Storytelling

The sharing of stories is as essential to public speaking as it is to romancing. Anyone can learn to tell an engaging story. It's as simple as reciting the alphabet. And it's a great way to impress your audience when giving a speech.

Creating a Storyboard

All good stories begin as elements put together in storyboard fashion. The storyboard may consist of different pages in a notebook, on a flip chart, or as separate sequences in the storyteller's mind. Regardless, the storyboard lays out the progression of the narrative. The storyteller must begin by setting the stage and introducing the characters and the conflict. The body of the story must build to a climax and achieve a resolution of that conflict. The conflict can be introduced immediately or foreshadowed to increase the suspense and intrigue. Try to have the audience worry along with your characters and care what happens next.

As the suspense of the story builds, you can certainly insert aspects for comic relief. However, you must approach the climax by building the tension. There should be the promise of exciting things to come, with curiosity aroused, uniting your listeners in anticipation. Thus you cannot give away everything in the introduction, but rather must keep up a certain amount of mystery, anticipation, and surprise.

Nothing captures our attention like a good story, well told. The listeners want to hear more and, no surprise, they become less aware of time as it passes in their capacity as listeners.

The Three Ms

To excel at the art of telling stories, it is important that we begin with the notion that a good story must satisfy each of the *Three Ms:*

It must be *meaningful.*
It must be *memorable.*
It must be *moving.*

Each of these is essential. The story must have a point in order to communicate meaningfully to the listeners. Stories as non sequiturs will fail. Similarly, the story must be memorable, carrying with it all the elements that will engage the listeners and stick in their minds. Finally, the story must move the listeners to a new way of thinking about the point or the shared experience.

Naomi Rhode, the past president of the National Speakers Association, tells a story that exemplifies each of these qualities.

Ms. Rhode was on the island of Maui with her husband walking along an isolated beach looking across the channel at the beauty of Molokai. At one point she turned to take in the lovely view of the mountain peaks through a puffy cloud and noticed the beautiful pattern of the footprints they were leaving in the sand. Moments later a huge wave came rushing in and nearly wiped them off their feet. Then, as she looked down, she noticed the wave had totally obliterated their footprints in the sand. She turned to her husband and said, "We didn't make much of an impression on the sand, did we?" Quickly, but thoughtfully, he replied, "It was because we were not walking on high enough ground."

Ms. Rhode's story carries with it great meaning, sticks in our memory, and can move any audience. It illustrates such a simple point through a story we can see in our mind's eye.

One tells or shares a story because it can "take you somewhere." A story told in a moving way will leave a large imprint and makes a lasting connection.

In 1947, Jackie Robinson became the first African American to play major-league baseball. One could use many words to describe this historical event and to place it in the context of the racial prejudice existing after World War II. However, the significance of this event is imprinted on my mind through the following sportswriter's story.

Pee Wee Reese was the shortstop on the Brooklyn Dodgers when Robinson was brought up to that big-league club. Raised in the South, Reese grew up at the knee of Jim Crow and had just served in the segregated armed forces. But he showed his true character one day in Cincinnati, when the fans were hurling epithets at Robinson. Reese decided he had had enough. The Dodgers were on the field, and the players in the Reds dugout were shouting obscenities at Robinson. Fans were booing and cursing Robinson, who was standing at his position at first base trying to control his own anger. Reese called time-out and in a gesture that has become famous, walked across the infield, placed a hand on Robinson's shoulder in a very public display of friendship, and offered him a few words of encouragement. The great baseball writer Roger Kahn said that this gets his vote as baseball's finest moment.

This story, like any good one, transports the listeners to a different place, causing them to lean in for more. This is a very learnable skill. Let's turn to how to tell a tantalizing story, and later how to solicit stories from others and from your own life's experiences.

The ABCs of Good Storytelling

So how do you tell the enticing story? It is as simple as A-B-C. The story needs to be:

A for *apt*
B for *brief*
C for *chronological*

Also, as I will explain below, the story must avoid each and every one of the Three Ds.

A Is for Apt

Let's start with *apt.* To be apt, a story needs to be "pegged" to a particular point, message, or purpose of your presentation. You must ask yourself, "What is the point of this story?" Then ask, "Is it tied into my presentation?" For example, I often tell this story I borrowed from one of Charles M. Schultz's *Peanuts* cartoons:

Charlie Brown, Linus, and Lucy are all laying side by side on a hill, staring up at the sky on a cloudy day. Lucy turns to Linus and asks, "What do you see in the cloud formations, Linus?" Linus responds, "In that cloud, I see the profile of the famous sculptor Thomas Eakins. Over there I see an outline of British Honduras. And over there I see the stoning of Saint Stephen with the apostle Paul standing to one side." Lucy responds, "That was very good, Linus. What do you see, Charlie?" Charlie Brown shrugs and says, "I was going to say I saw a ducky and a horsy, but I changed my mind!"

This story humorously illustrates many points. Typically, I use it to assure my speech students that they should not be like Charlie Brown, but rather speak their minds and express their thoughts.

For a story to be apt, it must be localized and personalized to the listeners. Garrison Keillor performs his radio show in different cities, in advance reading the local papers to pick up on the local stories and news. By making references to such matters and stories, he makes each of his broadcasts more credible and more apt.

Perhaps the true ABC of storytelling is to think of the particular "audience before content." One should tell stories that are personal and adapted to address the members of the audience. It is essential to pitch the story toward the audience's point of view.

B Is for Brief

The next essential for our ABCs of storytelling is that a story be *brief.* The problem with most stories, and the reason they often inspire such groans, is that they seem interminable. Surprisingly, it is not the retelling of a good story that bores the listener (in fact, the opposite is true). The real problem is stories that seem never to end.

Imagine you are in a business conference listening to the following:

An ancient sailing ship was blown by ill winds into the Bermuda Triangle one night. The captain was a wily old sea dog who had three ways to handle terrible storms. It just so happens that the one he chose that stormy night could also work miracles in your business . . .

This brief introductory story compels you to keep listening. By paring the story down to its essentials and eliminating the clutter, you can overcome the seven-minute adult attention span. The value of a story is lost if the listeners' minds wander.

C Is for Chronological

The final component of the ABCs of good storytelling is that the tale must be chronological. Stories are told along a timeline providing sufficient detail and imagery to keep the listeners with you. It's only in the movies that they use flashbacks or flash-forwards.

The following story* exemplifies this important principle of good storytelling:

> Charles Lindbergh, the first aviator to fly solo across the Atlantic, was a private man. When the movie version of his flight, *The Spirit of St. Louis,* starring Jimmy Stewart, came to the theaters in 1957, Lindbergh tried to attract as little attention as possible. In fact, he, his wife, Anne, and their three youngest children slipped into Radio City in New York one afternoon to see the film. The film presents the enthralling drama of Lucky Lindy's long flight and the perils he faced en route. About halfway through the film, during one particularly tense moment in the flight, his eleven-year-old daughter Reeve clutched her mother's arm and whispered, "He is going to get there, isn't he?"

This story is to the point, brief, and chronological. It provides only those details that are necessary to telling the story. For example, it simply does not matter what the Lindberghs were wearing, where they went after the movie, or even how the movie fared at the box office (not well!).

Avoid the Three Ds

To tell the perfect story, one must also avoid the *Three Ds* that can prolong a story to the point of boredom:

---

*Source: A. Scott Berg, *Lindbergh* (New York: Putnam, 1998), p. 503.

- Digression
- Diversion
- Distraction

Digress Not

We all have had the experience of listening to a story that digresses, losing itself on the meandering side roads of the tale. For example, in our "wouldn't eat them eggs" story, it might be tempting to discuss in great detail the contents of the "Kind Word" seminar, the number of trucks parked outside the diner, the other items on the menu, the people sitting in the diner, or even previous times at which one had ordered similar meals. However, each of these digressions would take away from the story's essential point.

Divert Not

Diversions cause a similar fate. Rather than briefly telling a story and maintaining the listener's taut attention, too many communicators divert attention by telling two stories at once. Diversion is even more than a digression; it is the wholesale overlapping of stories. We have all heard storytellers, in the middle of their own story, divert to yet another story within a story. This, too, threatens the attention span of any listener.

Distract Not

It is also *essential* when telling a *great* story that one avoid distractions, whether internal or external. Therefore, one must concentrate on getting from the beginning to the end of the story in a sufficiently direct fashion, so one does not lose the listener in the process. So, for example, if there is a distraction in the room, the best strategy is to stay focused on the story. Similarly, one should avoid interruptions when telling a tight, compelling story.

The Dos and Don'ts of Telling Stories

Here are some proven suggestions on how to tell a story well. Apply these carefully to all anecdotes, jokes, and stories you tell.

Dos

- Know your story thoroughly before starting.

- Make no apology for the story or your ability to tell it. (See imperative number one on page 42!)

- Watch the length of your story.

- Be sure your story is appropriate to the listener or audience.

- Build up carefully to the punch line or climax. Be sure that everyone hears all the preceding words.

- Stop when you have finished.

Don'ts

- Don't draw out short, quick stories into lengthy ones.

- On the other hand, be careful not to cut short stories that require a build-up for the humor or moral.

- Don't explain or repeat the story point. This is useless and annoying.

- Don't build up the story too much at the beginning by saying something like "This is positively the best story I ever heard."

- Don't omit important early details. Never correct yourself by saying something like "Oh, I forgot to tell you . . ." This lets your listeners down.

- Don't give away the point of the story too soon.

- Don't be a "chain storyteller" or "chain joker." Give the other person a chance.

- Don't speak too fast. This is the primary cause for people losing the story line.

Deconstructing the "Wouldn't Eat Them Eggs" Story

Your story does not need to be a lengthy folktale or a formal story in order to compel the use of the ABCs. Using these elements, let's deconstruct the "wouldn't eat them eggs" story included earlier this chapter.

This story must be set in context, by "pegging" it to a point to be made. For example, it readily illustrates the point that there can be something refreshing about speaking your mind directly. Then the stage must be set and the characters introduced. We learn of Bruce and our attendance at the "Kind Word" seminar and our trip home, with sufficient descriptions of the truck stop café and the grizzled waitress. We make the points by chronologically describing the waitress's taking of our order, Bruce's pixieish response, and her return. The story reaches its climax (and illustrates its point) as the waitress announces that she "wouldn't eat them eggs" if she were Bruce. This resolves the conflict and satisfies the curiosity as to what "kind word" the Alice B. Toklas look-alike will offer at the end. The denouement of the story undoubtedly is told by describing the look on Bruce's face and reiterating the value of plain speaking. Stories in today's world are often short, but they still must follow the basic ABCs.

Verbal and Nonverbal Skills

The art of great storytelling requires both verbal and nonverbal skills directed at engaging the listener.

Verbal Skills

Verbal storytelling skills begin and end with a commitment to using vivid word pictures. When telling a story, one must paint a picture, so that it plays on the video screen of each listener's mind. One needs to see the truck stop café–its red Formica tables, truckers sitting at the counter–in order to follow the story in one's mind's eye.

In many ways, however, the words of a great story will appeal to the listener's other senses. You can describe the narrative, asking the listener to imagine sounds, tastes, scents, and even touches. The listeners can identify with these senses and compare them to their own experiences. Therefore, through exaggeration and emphasis, the storyteller brings the narrative alive. The waitress is an "Alice B. Toklas look-alike," and she has been working at the café since the "Huns took Rome." The exaggeration and emphasis, accomplished in words, make the story more memorable. These are the basic verbal elements of any engaging story.

Nonverbal Skills

There's another kind of "language" to storytelling: It is the nonverbal use of the voice and the body. At its core, you must be a salesperson for your story–telling the story with a personal animation and enthusiasm. These qualities are contagious and assist you in keeping your listener's rapt attention. As with all effective communication (see chapter 13, "Building Good Chemistry"), the story rises and falls with variety: variety of voice, volume, and inflection. The changes in these nonverbal channels will emphasize the story's main points and its progress.

The dramatic or comedic quality of a story depends on its pacing. Here, your tools are rate and pause. We've all listened to great storytellers or even joke tellers and understand that it's all in the timing. You can't even imagine a storyteller building suspense or arousing curiosity without pausing for effect at critical moments. Your words may paint a picture, but it is your voice and body that set the mood.

The most essential nonverbal skill, of course, is making a direct connection with the listeners through eye contact and body gesture. Never read a story; rather, you must connect with the audience through your eyes and facial expression. To do this, you must know your story thoroughly and see it unfold in your mind's eye as you tell it. If you visualize the story as you go, you will never get lost or feel compelled to read words you have written in advance.

Practice your story with a mirror. You can use a real mirror, a tape machine, or a video recorder. If you have video available, review yourself and your story in different modes. First, listen without the visual. Then watch yourself, without the sound. Only then should you watch the complete performance. In this way, you can isolate the potentially distracting nonverbal aspects of your storytelling.

Where Do Stories Come From?

Now that we have confirmed that stories are essential to effective communication and have taught the art of telling a compelling story, the trick becomes how to find and create these great stories. If you say to yourself that "you can never think of a good story," or worse, that "you never had anything interesting happen to you," you are mistaken.

Each of us has a wide variety of experiences in our family life, work life, school life, and elsewhere that is an absolute treasure trove for good stories. I want you to imagine there has been a video camera taping every moment of your life. Imagine further that each scene or anecdote could be retrieved on demand. If these scenes were reduced to a CD-ROM, you could do word and image searches, locating the great stories of your life, to be shared with others in future communications.

Family

We can rediscover family stories and build up our own repertoire by asking parents, children, grandparents, and friends for the stories of our lives. We can keep a story journal to record these interesting and provocative events as they occur. As we tell these stories over and over again, we can select those that are meaningful and memorable and moving. We can utilize what storyteller Donald Davis calls "prompts" to retrieve such stories, such as these: "Can you remember a time when you cooked something and it didn't turn out?" "A trip that didn't quite go as planned?" "Becoming sick at an inconvenient moment?"

There is probably no more fertile source of stories than family life and family history. In fact, families that are good at communicating develop a story "hall of fame" in which those enduring tales are told and retold, often from generation to generation: for example, the family trip when the car ran out of gas. Maybe it's sending your oldest child off to college. Or something as simple as your first pet or your first kiss!

The following story has been told and retold innumerable times around my family's dinner table and elsewhere. It is about my paternal grandfather, Harold Wagstaffe.

As a young married man with one child, Harold Wagstaffe was told he was being transferred to a faraway branch of the Bank of Victoria in Ashcroft, British Columbia. My grandfather insisted on first visiting this remote location, traveling by a train hugging the side of a mountain. He arrived to see an ugly, muddy, one-street town. As he walked toward the bank, a drunk came hurtling through the swinging doors of the saloon, an anonymous hand pushing him to land face first in the mud. Disgusted, my grandfather returned to the Bank of Victoria and announced his resignation. (In those days you didn't just decline a job move.) It was an act of courage and led to his relocation to California, where he eventually spent a career with the Bank of America, working with A. P. Giannini. But for this single, random act of courage, my grandfather's son (my father) never would have met my mom, who was living in San Mateo, California. If not for their marriage, I would not have had five siblings. And, of course, there would have been no litter of nieces and nephews.

But for my grandfather's courage, all these members of my family would not exist. We can all agree:"The hand that pushed that drunk from the bar . . . was the hand of God!"

Every story need not be of great family historical significance. Rather, it can also be a story in which family members themselves have participated and played a role. For example, here's one that amused me:

A few years ago, I received a notice in the mail from America Online that our account was being canceled. Knowing that I had paid every month's bill, I called the Internet provider, only to be told that the account had been temporarily canceled as a warning. Their records showed that during the previous month someone from our computer had visited a chat room within which offensive language had been used. I approached my then-thirteen-year-old son, Michael, and asked him if knew anything about the cancellation or its reasons, since he was the only one computer literate at the time. A typical teenager, Michael responded to the question with an inarticulate "I dunno." I responded by saying that it was my understanding that AOL had suspended the account because

someone on our computer entered a chat room containing offensive language. Michael again professed his ignorance, although
this time a bit more shakily.

Now you have to remember, as you reflect on my next question,
that I am a lawyer and that with cross-examination there is wide
latitude. I prefaced my inquiry with the statement that Michael
should be aware that AOL "knew" who it was because of the associated screen name (the individual's online identification). Faced
with such implicative evidence, Michael confessed to the crime.
However, with the moxie and hubris of a teenager, he shot one last
salvo: "But Dad, you're a First Amendment lawyer." I responded
promptly, "Not in this house, I'm not!"

This story, while having its origins in a moment of
family tension, has become one of our all-time intrafamily
favorites. It provides both suspense and humor. Needless to
say, Michael was not allowed in a chat room for the next
twelve months.

Work

Running your video camera will also record many stories from your work life. For example:

In my very first jury trial, I represented a young woman who had
been hit in a crosswalk by an automobile and had her hip dislo-
cated. It was a case that my firm had given me as a young lawyer
because I couldn't lose it, and I didn't. However, there was one
surprising moment during the trial. I called to the stand the treating
orthopedist to testify as to the seriousness of my client's injury. I led
him through her injury and post-trauma care. We then placed the
X ray before the jury on a lit-up screen as the good doctor testified for
nearly thirty minutes about the significance of the various shadings
and hairline fractures being displayed. He suddenly stopped, took
a closer look, and announced to the jury with no question pending:
"That's not Mary's X ray . . . it's someone else's hip!" It turned out

> he had been talking for almost thirty minutes about a hip disloca-
> tion of one of his other patients! The court reporter's transcript
> shows that I valiantly attempted to salvage this awkward moment
> with the following words: "Judge, I need to go to the bathroom."

I have used this story many times to illustrate that things can go wrong and that you need to adapt to changing circumstances. I have also used it to highlight the importance of preparation. It is a self-deprecating story and always gets a laugh.

School

One can also recapture great stories from school life. So many serious events take place during your school years that you can add to your story repertoire simply by "downloading" such memories. For example:

> When I was in law school, the law professors, just like Professor
> Kingsfield in *The Paper Chase,* would terrify their students in a
> Socratic dialogue. It was usually impossible to anticipate the ques-
> tions. In the first semester of my first year, one of my classmates,
> Randy Erlewine, decided to enhance the odds a bit. We were tak-
> ing Professor Milton Green's afternoon civil procedure class, and it
> was Randy's turn to recite that day. But Randy did something that
> no one else had considered; he went to Professor Green's separate
> morning class, which followed the same syllabus. When it came
> time for our afternoon class, Professor Green predictably called on
> Randy to tell us the meaning of the *Dice v. Akron* case. Randy
> paused thoughtfully, and said he thought it was the "mirror image
> of the *Erie* case" that we had read the day before. Professor Green
> squealed with delight that a student had so rapidly summoned the
> main point. Randy beamed and never disclosed his secret. Rather,
> he accepted the kudos from his fellow classmates, most of whom
> wanted him to be in their study group for the rest of the year!

Story Lending Library

One can also build up a repertoire of great stories by visiting the "Story Lending Library"—borrowing (with attribution) great stories from others. These can be from famous folktales, myths, religious stories, legends or literature. They can be about historical figures or events. Get permission to use these stories and tell them from your point of view.

For example, I have often retold the story of the 1984 Ronald Reagan–Walter Mondale debate. As you may recall, there had been a great deal of discussion in the public arena that perhaps President Reagan was a little too old to be running for a second term. People talked of him falling asleep at cabinet meetings and the like. At the debate, the questioner asked Ronald Reagan to address this topic. In typical Reganesque style he paused, smiled, and said, "I refuse to make my opponent's youth and inexperience a campaign issue." With this single, self-deprecating response, President Reagan defused the entire issue, never to be heard in the campaign again.

With permission, I borrowed the following story from a friend of mine.

One of my best friends, Brad Levin, lives in Denver with his wife and two daughters. His younger daughter, Robyn, was at school in the month of December when Santa Claus made a surprise visit, asking each child to come up and tell him what he or she would like for Christmas. When Robyn got her turn, she sat on Santa's lap and was asked what she wanted for Christmas. Robyn responded, "We're Jewish, so we don't celebrate Christmas." Thinking fast, Santa said, "Well, you must know someone who celebrates Christmas, so please tell me what I could bring them for the holiday." Without guile and thinking of the Levin's live-in au pair, Robyn responded, "Well, we do have a Christian in the basement!"

Your challenge is to keep an inventory of great stories. If you concentrate just a little on remembering (and recording) the great ones, you will have literally hundreds of excellent stories to share with others as you romance the room.

Conclusion—Modern-Day "Campfires"

For countless centuries, shared stories have provided connections between people. Before there were movies, radio, television, or the Internet, people told stories to inform, entertain, and persuade. The word "bonding" may have its origins in the pop psychology of the late twentieth century, but it started in ancient days the first time someone told a story around a campfire.

Storytelling is as important to the corporate executive or salesperson as it was to prehistoric cave dwellers eating that night's meal around a fire. As listeners, we love the development of plot and character, the climax and the resolution. If you can gather and tell great stories to illustrate your presentations, you will leave every room with applause and appreciation.

STORYTELLING CHECKLIST

THE ABCs

→ Is your story apt?
→ Do you have a goal for your story?
→ Is your story brief?
→ Have you taken out all the unnecessary details?
→ Is your story chronological?

THE THREE Ds

•➤ Do you intend to digress from your story?

•➤ Do you intend to divert from the story?

•➤ Is there anything that will distract from your story?

THE THREE Ms

•➤ Is your story moving?

•➤ Is it memorable?

•➤ Is it meaningful?

OTHER FACTORS

•➤ Did you create a storyboard?

•➤ Have you thought about the verbal and nonverbal aspects of this story?

•➤ Have you started compiling stories in a journal?

CHAPTER 12

The Family Room

We have seen so far that there can be many challenges when romancing rooms in business, educational, and other "real-world" settings. However, for most of us, our world becomes most real when we are at home interacting with our families.

In chapter 4, we talked of the need for "shared meaning" when addressing an audience. In many ways, we are all looking for shared meaning when we speak with our families, comprehending the same language and ideas. Yet we often take family members for granted, leaving our communication skills at the front door to our "family rooms" and forgetting how vitally important it is to romance this room as well.

If it's the two-year-old child we're talking about, skilled communication requires verbal consistency, steadfastness, and a sense of humor in the face of the never-ending storm of nos. As children get older, romancing skills call upon your ability to display joy, to make clear what you want, and to set reasonable limits—while simultaneously sharing family stories and planting the seeds of the values you hope will flourish when you're not there to tend the garden.

When I'm not teaching or practicing law, I spend my time with my family—my wife and our four active children, who are winding their way to and through the teenage years. Although I'm a communication specialist, I find that one of the hardest things for me, and I think for any parent, is talking and listening to your growing children. A variety of questions always spring to mind during these sessions: Are they getting it? Are they even hearing me? Are we engaging in a conversation at all? Are they listening? Am I really listening?

When communicating in the family room with a spouse or children, most of us would love to have a miniature screen on the family member's forehead scrolling the thoughts they're really thinking, thoughts not always reflected in their words. If only this device existed, particularly when you are having a "conversation" with your teenager. As I renavigate the teen years (this time from a parent's perspective), there are times I would give anything to understand what is truly going on in my kids' minds and to have a conversation on any topic other than that night's curfew.

In the long-running television program *St. Elsewhere,* the main character, Dr. Westphal, had an autistic ten-year-old. It was an ongoing plot line that the child could not form interactive relationships with others, especially with his more formal physician father. In the show's final episode, however, Dr. Westphal had a dream that his son wasn't autistic anymore, and that they were conversing, sharing laughter, and even playing catch. The doctor awoke in the night after the dream, frantically found some scratch paper, and wrote it all down. After going back peacefully to sleep, Dr. Westphal woke up the next morning and looked at the sheet of paper, which contained only one word: "Life."

It is not a futile dream to hope for improvement in the

quality of communication within our families. Happily, the romancing techniques we have explored thus far—gaining favorable attention, listening while you talk, and avoiding distractions—apply to communications in our family rooms as well.

When I wrote this chapter, I thought it worthwhile to remember what it was like when I was a kid growing up. In search of inspiration—and a visual aid—I went to the family photo album, searching for a picture of me at the age when my conversations with my parents consisted primarily of phrases such as "You don't understand me." "You're not listening to me." "You don't know what it's like." And there I was—the third one from the right in the back row of my eighth-grade class. The picture hung on the family bulletin board when I was thirteen. If you look closely you can see there are pinholes all through my head. This is because I have five siblings, one or several of whom apparently thought it would be appropriate to turn my face into a pincushion.

The photograph (and some reflection) brought me to the point of remembering what it felt like to be a kid. If you're lucky enough (and I'm not) to have an old childhood diary around, the angst and bad writing will resurrect the memories even more clearly. As I reviewed this period of my youth, I remembered times I felt isolated and alone. I also had little (actually, no) understanding for the level of risk caused by certain behaviors—whether it involved driving, drugs, or sexuality. I know now, but didn't then, that virtually all my peers, when speaking to their parents, were saying or thinking, "You don't understand me."

Looking though such writings and viewing old photographs reminds me how utterly solipsistic kids, particularly teenagers, can be. Solipsism—seeing the world from a self-centered point of view—has a direct impact on communications in the family room. Romancing not only can seem difficult, it can seem impossible.

But the challenge no doubt is the greatest during the teenage years. For the parent striving for engaging communications, it can be depressing to see the morose, non-interactive child at home instantly transformed into an enthusiastic, energetic human being when a friend calls or sends an e-mail. You wonder if you are the only parent who has a kid trying out for the role of Jekyll and Hyde in the play of life.

Teenagers also want to go to parties, drive late at night, and watch R-rated movies with absolutely no restrictions whatsoever. That's because they've come to the conclusion they're smarter than you, and hypothesize that your logic and rules are not worthy of their consideration.

Romancing with Pathos

To break through the barriers that can be erected between family members, we must apply the first essential romancing rule for communicating within the family: It's rarely the logical that works, it's the pathos.

You will remember from chapter 4's discussion of how to court an audience that there are three types of "proofs" one can use when communicating your ideas to others: *logos, ethos* and *pathos. Logical* communication involves reasoning from one premise to another. You know: "The reason you shouldn't drive ninety miles an hour is because it endangers your life and is against the law." That's entirely logical—and at times ineffectual in the family room as the kids pass through adolescence to adulthood.

Ethos is a form of proof that relies on the inherent credibility of the source. Such communications, while working well with children whose age falls within the single-digit range, can fail miserably when applied to older kids. "You must do this, *because I say so*," parents are often heard to say. We often fall back on the use of such ethical communications, even though they are often ineffective.

Then there's *pathos*. These are communications based on emotional appeals. For example, the driver's education film *Red Asphalt* is still a benchmark in some areas because it has the greatest visceral impact. Cars are crashed, bodies are mangled, and skin is literally disconnected from the injured people's faces. The emotion-based appeal to the fear of pain and destruction works and is memorable. There is nothing abstract (or particularly logical) about this film. The gruesome images haunt the viewer; even teenagers don't want that to happen to them.

So, when you approach romancing the family room, you must work on engaging your kids (and your spouse for that matter) on emotional levels, always listening while you talk to what they're saying to you verbally and nonverbally. In this chapter, I address how family stories and the ritual exchange of family lore can deepen these connections, even if they seem invisible during the teenage years. My friends assure me that our teenagers will reappear and interact with us when they reach their twenties. For it is only then that they realize you as parents and caregivers are not as dumb as they once thought. I can't wait.

The use of pathos for communicating in the family also means that we must connect on an emotional level. For example, when a child comes home with a subpar grade, you can bring your own reaction to bear—which will probably ensure a slammed door—or focus on what the grade represents to the child: "Do you believe you deserved this grade?" "What were your reactions when you opened the report card?" Such open-ended questions directed at the emotional underpinnings of the situation have a greater chance of success than a stern lecture on the impact of the grade on the kid's future.

When questions are warranted, avoid the pointed variety. After trying cases for so many years, I've learned that if you want to find out anything helpful about a potential juror during the selection process, you need to use open-ended questions—not "Are you willing to be fair to my client, who is a large newspaper company?" but "Tell me, what do you think of newspapers?" The latter type of question opens us to a discussion, rather than a monosyllabic response.

Still, the Q&A method of communication has inherent drawbacks. Every parent has asked a variant of the following question in the family room over the years: "So, how was school?" The inevitable answer: "Fine." Rewording to inquire if "anything happened at school" evokes the even less fulfilling "nothing" response.

More often, you find out about your kids and improve your communications when there is no assigned topic for the question-and-answer session. Try settings where there are no questions at all. Open the channels for communication by increasing the opportunities for interaction. Think of your kid's or your spouse's interests and favorite activities; offer to join them, and then watch how they'll initiate a discussion on a formerly "forbidden" topic. Of course, this may require communicating in motion, particularly with older children who are constantly on the move.

But romancing in the family setting often is not easy, and suggestions like those made above may not work when applied to what you perceive as the frenzy or war zone of your home. Frustration can also easily set in when you try and try, only seemingly to be rebuffed by an angry or disinterested tone.

Not Taking Unromanced Responses Personally

Not only must we keep talking and listening despite the perception of failure, we must strive *not to take unromanced responses personally*. If it makes you feel any better, your loved ones don't really mean it personally. They're usually lashing out at a series of other things.

William Faulkner's promise that we will not only endure, we will prevail, should be a motto for modern parents. Our kids are railing. They can be angry and lonely. They must confront a world that provides access to drugs, sex, and incivility. If, however, we are to communicate with them successfully, and participate in such a romance for the long term, we must talk to them about these tough topics, and let them know they are not alone. Looking at the social labyrinth through which our kids must maneuver, you may gain more sympathy for the way they live.

There is no question that the level of discourse on television, in movies, and on the Internet has deteriorated. Whether it's on the radio in the car, or on cable at home, there seems to be little value given to keeping a civil tongue in your head. Unfortunately, this worsening of the language and civility of our culture has descended into our familial communications. Thus, it is far more common for a child or even a spouse to communicate in angry tones and use personalized, if not downright profane, language.

Kids and many adults have lost respect for the power and use of civilized and romancing language. It's cool to use swear words. But it is worth it to maintain rules of civility in our communications, even if it seems to be a losing battle. Romanced language leads to romancing. My mother repeated the "If it's not nice, don't say it" bromide so often, it became second nature to me. But we're dreaming if we think this is always going to be a twenty-first-century reality. Often we are forced to listen to the meaning behind the tone.

The best we can hope for is to provide a verbal model for our children. I don't mean just the "swear words equal a poor vocabulary" lesson. I mean that our own commitment to the elegance and euphony of language can affect—even if not immediately—the manner in which our children will communicate with others.

Taking Time to Talk Using the 3 Cs

It is important, then, when romancing the family room that one not yell and berate, but rather listen and talk. Talking to our family members is the key. The depressing fact is that *the average parent spends just 38 minutes a week with his or her child.* This averages out to 5.4 minutes per day. Compare this to the statistic that the average child watches 3.5 hours of television a day. In light of such statistics, we can hardly take it personally if our kids talk to their friends more than they talk to us. It's inevitable.

The trick to talking effectively with family members can be separated into what have been called the Three Cs: *compassion, comprehension,* and *connection.* These compose the bedrock of any romantic relationship.

Compassion

There can be so much passion in family communications. The task is to talk and listen with *compassion;* that is, with empathy and understanding. Then there is the added challenge of accepting the possibility that your compassion won't always be well received.

For example, a teacher calls to report that your child hasn't handed in a paper. You approach your child, and he tells you he lost it. It's natural to say, "You LOST it??!! Can't you keep track of anything?" It's natural to communicate *criticism*, but that is not one of the Three Cs. Family members will not confide in you if they feel that you are constantly judging them.

A more compassionate response might be "Oh, what a bad break, you lost your paper." This allows the child to express his or her ideas and feelings, rather than answer to your pointed rhetorical quetions. Interacting with compassion does not mean condoning another's misconduct and mistakes. Rather, one can stress the constancy of values (e.g., punctuality, responsibility) without engaging in a judgmental attack. Romancing demands courtesy.

Try the following compassionate phrases:

- It must be tough that...
- You must really be (nervous, scared, thrilled, excited, etc.) about...
- I can understand ...
- I know you're feeling (bad, anxious, etc.) about ...

The difficult part is to avoid following the compassionate phrase with the word "but"—for example, "It must be tough working this weekend on your term paper, BUT if you'd started on it last week, you wouldn't be in this mess." The critical lecture serves only to disconnect us from our family members, with very little gratification for us in the process.

Comprehension

The next C is *comprehension*. Comprehending the communications of your family members requires giving them your undivided attention and spending the time to listen to their interests and needs.

Comprehension requires that we observe and acknowledge the feedback from our children and spouses. It's really no different than speaking to an audience in a public setting. As we explored in chapter 3, "The Wandering Eye Syndrome," you must be alert to the signs of distraction, annoyance, and disinterest. If you "listen" to these reactions as well as the content and tone of your family member's communication, you will increase the chances of comprehending what the other person is really saying.

It's no wonder that broken family relationships suffer from a universal characteristic: The participants say that the other person never *listened* to them. Of course, effective listening means turning off the television or putting down the newspaper when someone wants to talk. It also means using all the well-trod communication techniques of active listening–for example, body facing the other, nods and words of acknowledgment, and repeating back the statements to let the other person know you've been paying attention.

Listening also means keeping an open mind to the other person's point of view. If we assume disagreement, it guarantees a disconnection. I had a highly contentious case some years ago that was assigned to a judge for settlement. After each group met with the judge in separate rooms at the outset, he later gathered the two parties together and told us this case could certainly be settled. The lawyers were mystified since we each assumed the other side's position was unreasonable. Quite to the contrary, the judge informed us that we must not have been listening to each other, because the plaintiff's settlement demand was for less money than the defendant was willing to pay!

Comprehension also requires that we show genuine interest in the other person's ideas. Try asking your family member questions like: "What would you do in this situation?" "How would you handle this?" "Do you think I'm reacting properly to this situation?" You are welcoming explanation and explication.

Comprehension is most difficult during times of crisis

and conflict. It is hard to be sympathetic and understanding when your child comes home three hours past curfew without having called in advance. If you discover that your child has been to a party where drugs or alcohol were present, restraining yourself from yelling is hard enough; comprehension at that moment seems virtually impossible.

The romancing technique is to discuss such controversial subjects earlier and often. Try posing hypothetical topic starters on a tricky subject, such as: "What would you do if you were at a party and someone brought in a keg of beer without the parents' knowledge?" "If someone offered you drugs and your friends all seemed to be partaking, what would you do?" In this less-charged setting, where there is less defensiveness, family members can talk about the subject.

I often represent members of the news media seeking to obtain public records from various agencies. When they call me to say that a particular agency is denying them access to documents, I know we've already hit a point of conflict. That is *not* the time to negotiate a protocol or policy for the exchange of such information. Rather, the time to sit down and discuss this subject of interest to these two groups with ongoing relationships is when there is no dispute. Without the heat of conflict, there can often be an enlightened solution.

Building comprehension into a family relationship works in much the same way. Too often we communicate only in punishment situations. We need to communicate when reward—not punishment and judgment—is possible. The reward is a more romanced relationship in which the family members better understand each other.

Connection

The third C is *connection*. In order to connect with members of your family, you must make them feel that their interests and needs are important. In chapter 4, we learned that connecting with others requires that you court the listeners and keep the "eye off the I." In other words, you must value *their* interests and experiences.

One of the best ways to connect with family members is to acknowledge their competence. Kids, in particular, are used to being told that they're incompetent. They're screwups. They're ruining things. They're making your life miserable. When my father got particularly frustrated, he'd say, "You've taken a year off my life!" This meant that he would have lived until he was 190 (as compared with the 78 wonderful years he did have) based on all the years my shenanigans took off.

In addition to acknowledging a child's competence, it is necessary to reward it. When I was a teenager, I thought that my brother Ray was getting unfair treatment. We both had a midnight curfew for weekend activities. Knowing he was going to be late, Ray would call at ten minutes to 12:00, report that he was going to be home at 12:30, and all would be fine. I would not call, and slip in at only ten minutes after midnight. I'd get in big trouble and Ray wouldn't–even though I was home twenty minutes before him. This experience did more than underscore the principle that it is better to ask for permission than to beg for forgiveness. My parents were rewarding my brother's competence for having had the responsibility to call in advance.

Connections within families are made in the context of daily communications. Peter Beagle, the great writer, wrote an article called "The Importance of Daily Love." In it, he said that one of the most challenging parts of life is to maintain appreciation for family members on a daily basis. We have a "shared vulnerability," Beagle wrote, that compels us to treasure the little communicative moments we have with each other. Not so easy with a teenager or angry spouse in the home–but just as necessary.

Some time ago, I had the most vivid dream that emphasized

to me the importance of daily connections. I dreamed that my brother Steve and I were at his house early on a Saturday morning. He said that Mom (who had been dead for a few years) would be there in one hour, prepared to spend the day with us. I spent that dream anticipating what we could do. I thought of everything—a picnic in the park, a talk about my kids, and asking for advice on family matters. Right as the clock struck the one-hour mark, and before Mom was there, I woke up. As I arose from this deep sleep, I realized each moment of that dream day with Mom would have been superb.

Not-So-Secret Tips for Romanced Family Communications

Take Long Trips Together

The confined environment of a family car trip can be an ideal setting for a romanced connection. I love these trips because when we're in the car, everyone eventually talks. In my family, we play games to make the time pass. There usually is some adventure or misadventure to add to our storehouse of family memories. We create the connection by engaging in a long-term activity together.

Good parents learn to find interests and activities that all family members can share. Make a list.

Establish Rituals

It is worthwhile to establish rituals in your family. For example, we have a "photograph day" on which we gather to look at family photos and talk about a silly memory we can look back on. On Memorial Day every year, we now gather to watch the film *Saving Private Ryan*. It is a pretty gory movie, especially for my youngest child. But my wife and I decided that it advances a positive value, and now it's become our tradition. Rituals give each member of the family a sense of belonging, as well as a common lore.

Family lore often times establishes a memory that binds family members for a lifetime. For example, my wife, Karen, takes one week off each year, leaving our four kids and me to fend for ourselves. However, each year she posts a color-coded chart on the refrigerator, specifying where each child is supposed to be at each minute of each day. Appropriately, she doesn't trust me for a minute. One year Karen got an intestinal illness on her trip and had to stay away an extra week recuperating. Now, here I was in week two—but there's no chart. So like in the movie *Groundhog Day,* I just repeated week one. The problem was that my kids' activities are different every week, and so I missed pickups, sent my daughter off in her Brownie uniform when there was no meeting, and pulled my hair out. But you know, we made it through, and that second week produced some of the best memories—and the best Dad jokes.

Celebrate Your Shortcomings, Not Theirs

Family members often feel that the parent or spouse revels in their shortcomings, almost enjoying the act of criticism. The opposite is better: Celebrate your own shortcomings. Talk about the challenges you've had and particularly your foibles. For example, I talk too fast. In my speech class they call me J-I-M, for "jaws in motion." I know this, and so I revel in the foible. I let my kids tease me about it, and many days it is the subject of an in-house roast. This brings us together, and lightens our load.

PART 3

Advanced Romancing the Room Techniques

CHAPTER 13

Building Good Chemistry

Some couples on a date seem well matched in theory, but the chemistry is missing. There is something about the way they interact that ends any chance for a second date. So, too, with romancing the room and communication skills: It's often not *what* we say, but *how* we say it, that nips a romance in the bud.

A large part of engaging others, therefore, depends on *delivering* presentations in ways that build chemistry with the listeners. Such chemistry requires the *use of verbal and nonverbal catalysts, avoiding the mixing of incompatible compounds, and ensuring positive and binding reactions.*

Verbal and Nonverbal Catalysts

If you want good chemistry, you must use stimulating verbal and nonverbal catalysts. You catalyze by varying your presentation to avoid monotone and boredom. Variety is one of the greatest tools we have as communicators: variety in voice, variety in word choice, and variety in gestures.

The Power of Your Voice

Your voice is a musical instrument, a beautiful musical instrument, its sounds made by air moving up with the contraction of the diaphragm. Like any good musical instrument, the voice creates the best effect when a variety of notes are played. I can play only one song on the piano: "Big Ben at Twelve O'clock." I press one key over and over again, twelve times. It's not a catalyzing song. If that were the only song you'd ever heard, you'd never realize what incredible music can come from a piano.

There is the same potential with the voice. You don't have to be a one-note speaker. Your voice has enormous potential for variety. You can pause. You can change volume. You can change your rate, your pitch, and your inflection. Using this variety will accomplish your goal of building good chemistry with the audience.

Inflection

Inflection can create meaning. As a communicator you must decide on where that inflection should be. Some of it will come naturally, of course, but a change in emphasis or inflection can dramatically affect meaning.

You can see how effective variety of inflection can be by emphasizing different words in this simple sentence: "The pie I baked." Say it out loud. Now emphasize the first word– "the." Actually, it becomes "thee" when you emphasize it. So now it is "*The* pie I baked." Then emphasize the word "pie"; it's a pie, not a cake. "The *pie* I baked." Next try: "The pie *I* baked." *I* baked it, nobody else. Finally say, "The pie I *baked*." I *baked* it. I didn't do anything else with it.

By engaging in this basic exercise you can see that variety of inflection changes meaning; it is an amazing technique you have available to you. You can take the same speech and deliver it in all sorts of ways.

Think of inflection like hearing a great song by two artists with completely different arrangements. A good example of this is Madonna's recent rendition of "American Pie." Her version is in many ways a different song than the original by Don McLean. The difference is in the inflection.

Pitch

Pitch is the musical quality of your voice. Do you speak in a low bass pitch or a high soprano voice? Do you keep your voice at the same pitch all the time, or do you vary the pitch of your voice from high to low? You can change the pitch of your voice to help bring definition and emphasis to your spoken words.

Rate

Variety of rate is easy. You can go very fast in a communication, or you can slow way down. You need to determine which is most effective for your particular communication.

The average presenter speaks at some 125 words per minute (approximately half a page of double-spaced typewritten words). However, the rate of effective speaking can vary from 75 to 225 words per minute, with the trick being to *vary* the rate within any given communication. It might produce excellent chemistry to quicken the pace of the dramatic part of a tension-filled story, but it's equally necessary to slow the pace noticeably when explaining the complexities of atomic particles.

Pause

Pause, while seemingly similar to rate, is actually quite different. Rate is the number of words you speak per minute; pause is where you choose to create a momentary silence. A three-second count is about as far as you should go with a pause, and that is only when you are really working to create effect. Generally speaking, your pause would be a one-second count or less. Varied pauses in a presentation not only refresh, they engage. The speaker is able to provoke thought with a carefully chosen pause after posing a rhetorical question; to arouse interest with a pause before presenting a story's climax; and to trigger laughter with a well-timed hesitation before delivering the punch line of a joke.

Filler Words

After you've got vocal variety down, watch out for ums and uhs. Using filler sounds makes you appear inarticulate. In a recent university publication, a linguistics column noted that the sound "uh" usually appears before a short delay in speech averaging 2.65 seconds. Think of that–almost a three-second pause follows every "uh." The ubiquitous "um" is followed by longer silences averaging 8.83 seconds. The linguist came to this conclusion by studying the conversations of thousands of people. All of this tells you that when you use filler sounds or words, you're not building good or dynamic chemistry with your crowd.

Filler words hurt the speaker's credibility and interrupt the flow of the communication. In our culture, here are the most common filler words or sounds:

- Um
- Uh
- And um
- Really
- You know
- Like
- Okay

The challenge when romancing a room with your delivery is to eliminate filler words and sounds from your spoken vocabulary. You can do it because we're in charge of our language. When I was a kid, I might have used profanity when in the schoolyard. However, around my father (who mysteriously told me that even "stud" was a dirty word), I never once used a vulgar word or phrase. Make your sounds count.

Volume

Volume is one of the great tools available to you as you use your voice. Your volume will vary, of course, depending on the setting.

When I am going to speak somewhere, I want to know everything about the room's accoustics, the microphone, the setting, and so on. For the environment you're in will affect your choice of volume. Is it a small, intimate room or a cavernous, echoing room?

Is the speech in the morning or the evening? Does it follow a meal, making staying awake more challenging? I will do my best to put pins under the listeners' seats to keep them awake, using varied volume as my device.

The Importance of Gestures

Sometimes your catalyzing agent will be your physical presentation. Think of the difference between having an erect, energetic posture, shoulders up and back, and slumping or slouching. Stand at the podium, don't lean on it.

Be graceful with gestures. Generally, when you gesture, your arms should move from the shoulder and not from the elbow. Moving from the elbow is a short and awkward movement. Like a dancer, a speaker's movement requires fluidity. Ask yourself these simple questions: Do my gestures get in the way? Are they distracting? Are they so nonexistent that the audience isn't even sure you are communicating with them?

There are certain fixed gestures you should avoid because they are awkward and static. One example is the "bear hug": arms across your chest. Another is the "military at ease," where you have your arms behind your back and you don't move at all. For the "one-armed bandit," one hand dangles loosely at your side while the other serves as a tourniquet above or below the elbow. Avoid the "firing squad," with your legs slightly spread, hands tied behind the back, as if you're about to be shot and the only thing missing is a bandanna over your eyes. Another problematic stance is the "choirboy/girl," which is hands at waist level, fingers entwined, and looking as if there's a table in front of you and you're resting your hands on it. That's not good for chemistry. The "supplicant" pose is similar to the "choirboy/girl" but has your hands placed higher up on your chest. With the "fig leaf," your hands are down at your crotch, guarding it. Finally, avoid the uninteresting "bishop's gesture," where your hands are in front of you like a church steeple, and you're tapping the tips of your fingers together.

Also be sure to avoid unproductive or overly emblematic hand movements. One example of this is "the Lady Macbeth," or hands wringing compulsively as if they're washing out a bloodstain. Another is "happy pockets": hands in your pockets, playing with change. This is annoying and the audience won't listen to you—just your change.

Mixing Incompatible Compounds

For a chemical compound to work, the elements must combine both efficiently and safely. Far too many speakers, however, mix oil with water, insensitively saying or doing things that are incompatible with the values or orientation of their listeners. Rather than romancing the room and building good chemistry, these speakers engage in *turnoffs* that combust the crowd with no possibility for later recovery. Turnoffs are words or actions that distract, or annoy, or pit the audience against you. These can involve profane, sexist, or even racist comments. And the audience (or at least certain of its members) may not let you know of your romantic faux pas; rather, it may just go cold, while holding its annoyance and anger for your post-speech review.

A public setting is never the appropriate venue for a joke laced with sexist or racist overtones. Terms that might not seem loaded or inappropriate in the steam room will offend a dangerously large percentage of people in public settings. Therefore, it is essential to avoid turnoffs and the destruction of good chemistry that result from insensitive or intemperate remarks. Run your stories, your jokes, and your phraseology by someone in the affected group, and ask him or her for a frank assessment of their propriety. Then follow that person's advice, because it's never beneficial to insult others–even if the perceived injury was unintentional. Use a thesaurus when describing bodily functions. You should avoid profanity completely. Why do something as a speaker that will turn off the audience? You don't need turnoffs.

I teach a First Amendment class. Every year I cover the *Texas v. Johnson* case, decided by the U.S. Supreme Court a decade ago, in which the court narrowly held that the citizens of this country have a constitutional right to burn the American flag. The first year I taught this class, I brought in a flag . . . and I lit up one corner. I had a constitutional right to do that. But I shouldn't have, because there were people there, three to be exact, who went to the dean's office and said they were offended that I had singed the flag in class. The next year I thought I had a better idea. I brought in a flag, but I didn't burn it; instead, I didactically wiped the board with it. That year, four people went to the dean's office. Clearly I was trying to make my point in a way that turned off my students; they weren't listening to me anymore. I still use Old Glory as my visual aid—but now I hold it with respect.

Positive and Connecting Reactions

To build chemistry you must ensure positive reactions by using techniques that connect you to the audience. You really don't want to speak when your audience is not with you. To keep your audience with you, you need to think about what will interest them and keep their attention.

People Examples

Listeners inevitably will react positively to examples. In fact, the words "for example" should be in every speech you deliver. And I've learned as a trial attorney that examples with people in them are the best kind. The witness serves as my example, and good ones really connect with the jury.

If I needed to prove that I work too hard, I'd use this example. My client was the *New Yorker* magazine. For three weeks before trial, I was at the office every night until after the kids went to sleep, leaving the next day before they got up. The trial went on for five weeks, and I kept up the same schedule. At the trial's end, I made my daily call home to say I'd be late. Emily, my then-nine-year-old daughter, answered the phone, saying, "Wagstaffe residence." I said, "Emily, may I speak to your mother?" And she said to me, "Can I ask who's calling?" I knew then I hadn't been home enough.

Engaging Facts

Another way to elicit positive reactions from your listeners is to provide engaging facts. For example:

- Babe Ruth hit 714 home runs in his career. But do you know how many times he struck out? 1,330 times.

- We have a dental decay problem right now in this country. There are presently 600 million unfilled cavities in the United States.

- I was born in the middle of human history, for the world of the mid-twentieth century is as different from today as it was from the time of the Neanderthal man.

Engaging facts can back up your point and connect you to your listeners. Sound interested in your facts, and make them come alive for the audience.

Connecting Quotations

Quotations are also very helpful for obtaining positive reactions from your audience. Oftentimes, I give speeches on a subject that seems very dull to many people–federal civil procedure. I gave one speech titled "Federal Civil Procedure, Hemlock, and Other Poisons That Can Kill You." In my introduction, I quoted Voltaire, who said, "There are no poisons, only bad stomachs." That's a connecting quotation, and it got a laugh.

When I'm giving a speech on a topic that involves changes, such as when the law has changed or has developed, I say, "It was the comedian Steven Wright who said that he was walking down the street wearing his glasses when his prescription ran out. You may feel like the prescription has run out on your glasses as you learn these new facts."

Common Allusions

As a speaker, you can get positive reactions by using common allusions; that is, making references to things you and your audience have in common. It might be a bestselling book. It might be the movie that's the hit of the summer. Maybe it's a popular television show. Maybe it's something from today's newspaper. This is what I call the *"Hey, yeah" experience,* as in: "Hey, yeah, I can identify with that." You'll find that the audience perks up at the common reference. If they're daydreaming or thinking of something else, the audience is right back with you when it hears a common reference.

Your job as a speaker is to find common allusions–items with which we can all identify. For example, you could make a reference to the TV show *Who Wants to Be a Millionaire?* Since this has been such a hit show, most everyone knows what you're talking about. The common allusion bonds the speaker with the listeners in a memorable way.

Achieving Proximity to the Audience

Like in molecules, the speaker's and the listeners' spatial arrangement often determines whether one can obtain the desired reaction. Skilled communicators achieve great chemistry through use of the physical and personal space available. This involves capitalizing on both the *proxemics* of the room and visual contact with the audience.

Proxemics

The way a speaker uses the physical space in a room is called *proxemics.* The communicator's relative proximity to the audience–a matter of deliberate choice in great speeches–can make the difference between obtaining energized or deadened listener reactions. Of course, a speaker should, if possible, vary his or her physical orientation to the crowd during a presentation. It may be as simple as taking a step to one side of the podium for emphasis, or as complex as selectively moving from spot to spot—as well as standing, leaning, and sitting for effect during a long lecture. There's a reason why Oprah Winfrey and other skilled talk show hosts physically work the room—it ensures good chemistry during the day's taping.

The choreography of movement during a presentation is a true art. For example, most speakers agree that one moves closer to an audience when making personal points and appeals. In contrast, the speaker stands farther away when playing more of an entertainer's role. The distance permits the more voluminous and sweeping gestures that are consonant with the performer's objective. Thus, a preacher delivering a "hellfire and brimstone" sermon often will remain at a distance, behind the pulpit; whereas the cleric striving for a more intimate appeal to personal values might come into the congregation itself.

Take the traditional theater. When a scene is highly dramatic or comic, the actors stand behind the proscenium arch, distancing themselves from the crowd to enhance the performance. However, when there is a soliloquy or a comic aside, the actor often steps beyond the "fourth wall" and speaks while physically closer to the audience, creating a mood of intimacy. The variety in the use of space makes the play more engaging.

Of course, too much or uncontrolled movement can distract the audience from the speaker's points. If you pace to and fro, or constantly rock back and forth, you draw attention away from the speech, placing the focus on the annoying and repetitive proxemics. Many an audience member has been known to say that they were actually *tired* after listening to one of those so-called motivational speakers traverse the stage for hours. Balanced and thoughtful movement is preferred.

Visual Contact

As discussed in depth in chapter 6 on "Romancing the Fly," eye contact may well be the speaker's greatest tool for connecting with the audience. You work the room visually, entering the listeners' personal space with your eyes. Your eyes read your listeners' reactions and moods, while engaging them with your presentation.

There's a long list of speech elements that simply *cannot* be read from a written text or card. These include: a story, a rhetorical question, any use of the first person plural ("we") or second person singular ("you"), the presentation's introduction and conclusion, any personal appeals, and virtually all special-occasion talks (such as toasts). The loss of visual contact destroys the chemistry and eliminates the desired dramatic or comedic reaction.

I'm often asked if this means that speakers–unless they have the rare luxury of a teleprompter–must forgo the otherwise great benefits of using notes or a textual speech. To believe that this is true would consign all audiences, formal and informal, to the vagaries of purely impromptu speeches for eternity. Perish the thought!

Reading a Speech While Fully Engaged

Long before the teleprompter, great orators from Winston Churchill to Franklin D. Roosevelt were able to deliver prewritten speeches while maintaining eye contact with their audiences throughout their presentations. To know how this can be accomplished, you must learn the art of reading a speech while remaining fully engaged. It's called the "snapshot method," and it's based on the principle that *you must never read and speak at the same time.*

The object of the snapshot method is to look down at the text of the speech, capture a phrase, and deliver it after looking up at the audience. The trick of this technique is to *break up the text into readable snapshots.* Rather than typing your speech in long, single-spaced prose extending from margin to margin, you prepare your text in photographical images, readily captured in brief glances down at a well-proportioned page.

For example, the beginning part of the Gettysburg Address might be presented visually as follows:

"Fourscore and seven years ago
our fathers brought forth, on this continent,
a new nation,
conceived in liberty,
and dedicated to the proposition
that all men are created equal."

The speaker glances down and photographs the phrase, and *then* looks up and delivers it to the audience. If the pause breaks are well chosen, the next photographic glance downward will go unnoticed as the speaker prepares to get the phrase and look up and deliver it with gusto.

The impediment many presenters confront when delivering prepared speeches is that the actual written text is so packed together and condensed that the snapshot method is virtually impossible. In contrast, the readable text should be at least triple spaced, and in large and even varying or colorful fonts so that the "snapshot" will be quick and efficient. This eliminates the "losing your place" panic that can interrupt an effective snapshot-then-delivery style.

To enhance my delivery, I also underline key words, and double underline for greater emphasis. I will specifically mark my text with slash marks for a pause, and use double slash marks for a two-count pause. Even when I speak with the aid of a teleprompter, I still insist on bite-size phrases for easier reading and delivery. And when practicing (which gives me a rehearsed visual cue for the location of phrases and page breaks), I even employ "stage directions" for delivering particular phrases and stories (e.g., "slow," "strong," "with smile," etc.).

When all is said and done, I will have built good chemistry with my listeners because I have made the physical and visual connections that will keep their attention and enhance their understanding of my presentation. To paraphrase the age-old advertisement, it means better romancing through good public-speaking chemistry.

CHAPTER 14

Being Spontaneous: The Ten Commandments of Impromptu Speaking

Once I thought I was scheduled to give a brief toast as part of a dinner program honoring a retiring judge. At least that was the intent conveyed to me before my arrival. As I looked over the program, to my astonishment, I read that James Wagstaffe was the keynote speaker for the night. This came as a complete surprise to me! I hastily excused myself from the preprogram, went into a side room, and composed my "keynote" address. Sometimes even best-laid plans go awry.

Seldom do we plan these types of situations, or even our casual conversations, in advance. We wing it from the seat-of-our-pants based on our knowledge and experiences. Generally this will suffice with our friends and families, but often, like in a good romance, we are in spontaneous situations where speaking off-the-cuff becomes an awkward test of our communication skills. It might be giving an unplanned toast at your wife's sister's wedding, a short presentation at the parent's association meeting, a brief opinion at the monthly marketing meeting, an entertaining story at a business dinner party, or filling in for an associate running late. The possibilities are endless.

People compliment me on how well I speak in impromptu settings. Little do they know the extent to which I personally dislike being an off-the-cuff speaker. I don't always think that well on my feet. Through the years I have developed a series of tools for helping offset the discomfort of being put into these spontaneous situations where I have to romance the room.

Some of my friends thrive on these impromptu situations and excel at being the life of the party. They, too, are often not completely pure extemporaneous speakers. They are constantly preparing a short joke and interesting stories, hoping to entertain and inform their listeners. They try to slip them in at appropriate times. Frequently they are actually prepared extemporaneous speakers. This is a form of contrived spontaneity. It is not that difficult to become a seasoned impromptu speaker, but there are a few tools you need to learn to use. I call these the Ten Commandments of Impromptu Speaking.

Commandment One: Calm Down

Commandment number one is the most important commandment of all public speaking, particularly in impromptu speaking. Commandment one is to *calm down.* Dissuade yourself from letting the experience overwhelm you. Calm down, think clearly, and focus on communicating succinctly. You'll have up to fifteen seconds to pause in any speech before people become impatient with the silence. Besides, silence is one of the greatest attention grabbers. People will stop and look up at the speaker to find out what's happening.

Often in these spontaneous situations we let our internal monitor get the best of us. This is the little voice inside that is constantly asking, "How am I doing?" "Oh my God, I forgot what I am going to say next." "If only I could remember that company's or that person's name." Initially you need to silence this internal monitor. The way to do this is to merge this internal monitor into one communicator. Stop trying to dissect your speech while it is in progress. This is much easier to do if you follow the next three commandments.

Commandment Two: Pick a Purpose

The second commandment is to *pick a purpose.* Your general purpose is always to entertain, inform, or persuade, but what is your particular purpose? What are you trying to accomplish with these spontaneous remarks? What are the basic points you want to make? Outline this quickly in your head. This is half the battle.

In my speech class at Stanford University, I have an exercise in which each student comes to the front of the class, picks a word out of a hat, and speaks on this topic for five minutes. This is a variation of my father's after-dinner drill of giving a child a topic and saying, "Okay, stand and talk." The topics in my class have ranged from moose to pretzel. The student blindly picks a card, calms him- or herself, and speaks.

The purpose of each of these impromptu speeches was completely different. The point is this: after calming yourself, define your purpose. Make sure your listeners know your purpose for speaking. Use pauses strategically to calm yourself and define your purpose. Don't ramble on and on and have your listeners thinking or, even worse, saying, "And so, what's your point?" Be clear. Pick a purpose!

Commandment Three: Pick an Introduction

The third commandment is to *pick an introduction* once you have calmly established your purpose. Decide what your first words are going to be. How are you going to introduce this speech? What are you going to say? Remember, the introduction to a speech is designed to get the attention of the audience so it will listen closely to what you are saying. Start with a bang!

Now, pick the introduction. It could be a story. It could be an illustration. It could be a quotation. It could be a phrase that leads into the rest of the speech. Whatever form it takes, it has to be an introduction. Your introduction should segue directly into the purpose of your speech. It should not be a non sequitur. Many people like to start a speech with a funny story—a story that has no relevance to the speech. They've heard that is what you are supposed to do. That is *not* an introduction! That is a separate speech! An introduction must fit the purpose of the speech and lead the audience to the thesis or topic.

Your introduction should be something simple. Some people, consciously or unconsciously, make their introductions complicated. Lawyers are notorious for doing this. I know, I've had to hear countless complicated introductions in my career. In our pretzel example, the introduction might be as simple as this: "Walking to class tonight, on this wonderful spring day, I strolled by my favorite place in all of Palo Alto ... the pretzel stand right there on University and Ramona."

Okay, so you have calmed down, picked a purpose, and made your introduction. That's all in the first thirty seconds of your spontaneous speech.

Commandment Four: Pick a Pattern of Organization

The fourth commandment is hard to follow the first time you try it, but as you practice, you will get better at it: *Pick a pattern of organization.* You are generating this speech on the fly. You need to be organized! So pick a pattern of organization that lays out naturally with the thoughts you want to convey. Then it is easy to fill in the gaps.

There are a number of patterns of organization. One of the easiest is *the time pattern.* Take a topic, speak about its history, then discuss the present situation, and finally speculate on the subject's future. If you pick this organizational pattern, you will know exactly where the speech is going.

The time pattern works well with many topics, but it may be easier to organize your thoughts in *order of importance.* Talk first about the most important aspect of the topic and work down to the least important. Conversely, talk from the least important aspect to the most important.

If you use this pattern, be sure *not* to sound like you're reading off a list: "Another thing is ... and another thing is ... and another thing is ..." This is not a pattern! It is just a rambling list that is not public speaking.

Great speeches are tested by how well one idea transitions to the next. A good speaker will carry you from one point to the next with an organized and meaningful transition. If you say, "Well, another thing is ..." you are introducing a potentially unrelated item. But if you move from a less important point to a more important point in your speech using a well-placed connecting phrase, your listeners can follow your argument much closer and see where you are going with the speech.

We have talked about time and importance. How about place? Maybe your particular topic will lend itself to *different geographic perspectives.* How do Europeans regard this topic? How do Americans react to the subject? How do people in Australia respond to this? If you are giving a political speech, you should talk about that issue or candidate from different regional perspectives.

Now, these are just sample forms of pattern. Someone who I competed against when I was in school had the same introduction for every impromptu he ever delivered. If you heard him round after round, it got a little old, but to each person who heard him for the first time, he sounded downright brilliant. Whatever the current events topic was, he would say, "The whole world is a forest. And in this forest there are rabbits and there are wolves." He would break the impromptu subject into rabbits and wolves. Whatever he spoke about, he presented the subject from either the rabbit's view or the wolf's view. I thought it a little corny, but it does illustrate the point of your need to organize your speech—and provide a good introduction.

The pattern of organization is very important to impromptu speaking. It gives you a direction to go and keeps you out of trouble. You can avoid your greatest anxiety—the fear of going blank—by invoking the fourth commandment: using a pattern of organization to pull you along.

Commandment Five: Use Supporting Materials

The fifth commandment is to *use supporting materials.* Don't just make points in your speech; illustrate your points with a story, an example, or a visual aid.

Frequently an impromptu speech sounds like a prepared speech. How can that happen? Students of communication begin to develop a repertoire of interesting supporting materials. These materials can be good verbal illustrations, meaningful quotes, touching personal stories, or classic examples. You should mentally have these at your fingertips to draw upon in any speaking situation. As you continue to practice the art of public speaking, you will develop this library of supporting materials. You can become a raconteur by drawing on these bits of supporting information, stories, and illustrations at the drop of a hat.

Commandment Six: Pick a Conclusion

All right, you have made it though the first five commandments! The *sixth commandment* is to *pick a conclusion!* The speech has to end, and it's you who has to bring it to a close. You introduced the speech. You presented your organized thoughts in a cohesive pattern using supportive materials along the way. The speech has built to an engaging crescendo, and now it is time to make your concluding statement. Of course you're going to end before expected, but before you end there needs to be a final statement. We don't want this speech to just fade away into nothingness. Ideally, to paraphrase T. S. Eliot, you end with a bang, not with a whimper. Don't just end by saying, "Well, I guess that's my speech . . ." That's not an ending! You need to create a great ending—a memorable ending.

There are different kinds of conclusions. The *summary* is a simple one. This is what is used in the classic military approach to communication. You tell the audience what you are going to speak to them about, you speak, and then you reiterate what you just spoke about.

Audiences like to have cues. They have expectations that need to be met. The phrase "And in conclusion . . ." is a cue to the audience that you are coming to the end of the speech. Don't ramble on for another ten minutes after you've told your listeners you're about to end. It violates the audience's expectation.

There is also the *capsule conclusion,* in which you go back to your introduction, which now encapsulates the speech. You come back to the introductory words. We in the audience now have the cue; we know the speech is ending because the speaker has gone back to the introduction.

When I was in high school, I won awards with a speech titled "Instantism." The concept of instantism was that we are all running our lives in a time-paced manner. (By the way, this was in 1974, and the situation's gotten worse, not better.) What I proposed as a solution was relearning the ability to wonder. My ending was "As any five-year-old would tell you, to wonder takes time." Well, that was an ending, obviously, cued as an ending. You cue the ending with the way you word it as well. Get yourself to the point where you can end any speech. Don't just fade away.

Commandment Seven: State, Demonstrate, and Restate Your Point

Now let's go to *commandment number seven: State your point, demonstrate your point, then restate it.* When you are asked to exchange your ideas in a meeting, or when someone asks you a question in an interview, or wherever you're in any impromptu speaking setting, this methodology is a good way to express your thoughts. State your point. Demonstrate it or support it with the three basic forms of proof–logos, ethos, and pathos–or perhaps using supporting materials as the proof. Then restate your point. This is one way of organizing your speaking points. You need a pattern of organization, and then you use a variety of supporting materials so that your points can easily be stated, demonstrated, and restated.

Commandment Eight: Speak in Complete Sentences

Commandment number eight sounds easy, but is not always so. I know this from reading transcripts of speeches. You need to *speak in complete sentences.* If at all possible, try to speak in paragraphs, too. Avoid the tendency to digress syntactically. Keep your sentences relatively simple. Think about the way a sentence is constructed, as if what you say will show up in a transcript. Sentences should be constructed with a subject and a verb and occasionally an object, more often than not. It is that simple. When you start using the "whiches" and the "wherevers" and going off on digressions, you tend to lose the focus of your impromptu presentation. If you have time to write your speech out in advance, or think it out in advance, you can construct a great psychological model of a speech. This is a luxury not available when speaking impromptu. Discipline yourself to finish your sentences.

Ideally, speaking is like writing. Paragraphs have topic sentences that are explicated and lead to the next topic sentence. Try this method: Look at a transcript of your most recent speech. Take the topic sentence of each paragraph and eliminate everything else. See if the topic sentences tell the story you really want to convey. If they don't, then maybe your organization is not as logical as it should or could be.

The second thing to do is to take the end sentence of the paragraph and the beginning sentence of the next paragraph and eliminate everything else. How do they tie together? Test your transitions. Look at your topic sentences; do they tell the story? Do the ideas in the last sentence and first sentence of paragraphs lock into each other as you go? That is the ideal scenario, and hard to do in impromptus.

Commandment Nine: Use Speech Vehicles

Commandment number nine is to use what we call *speech vehicles.* A speech vehicle, unlike an organizational pattern, is an image or a word that carries the speech through. It is a motif, a recurring thematic element. For example, in Kurt Vonnegut's *Slaughterhouse-Five,* every time someone dies, the following phrase is used: "So it goes." The point of Vonnegut's description of the bombing of Dresden in World War II is that death becomes so commonplace, you begin to read through the repetitions of "So it goes." The phrase becomes the vehicle that makes the book more engaging and memorable. This kind of speech motif is just one of the things that you can do; it is hard to utilize in *every* impromptu, but sometimes this technique lends itself to the topic.

Commandment Ten: Use Your Topic as a Launchpad

Commandment number ten is to be used only when necessary: *Use your topic as a launchpad.* Let's say you are asked to speak on a topic that you know nothing about. That is a moment of great terror as a communicator. It is perhaps only matched by the terror of losing your place in your speech. What you must do in this situation is gather yourself. Then you can try using your topic as a launchpad.

A few years ago, someone in my speech class was given the topic "Nuclear Proliferation: Is It Still a Problem in Today's World?" Apparently he knew nothing about nuclear proliferation. He got up and said, "Nuclear proliferation: is it still a problem in today's world? You know, I know nothing about nuclear proliferation, but what I do want to tell you is this proves you should read the newspaper every day." And then he talked about the importance of reading a newspaper. To carry this technique off, you must create a connection between the topics. You are taking a topic and using it to get somewhere else. You can do that if the segue is appropriate enough. I wouldn't use it as a regular technique, but it does get you out of a tight spot when you are completely blank.

Learning to speak impromptu can be invaluable in so many careers. Like in a good romance, resourceful spontaneity in communication settings can charm and impress your listeners and ironically training to be spontaneous is the key.

IMPROMPTU SPEAKING REVIEW QUESTIONS

1. What is the first and most important commandment? _____
   _____

2. What must you do in order to stay calm and focused? _____
   _____

3. What are the characteristics of a good introduction? _____
   _____

4. What are some of the different patterns of organization
   in a speech? _____
   _____

5. How can you effectively illustrate your points and make an impromptu
   speech seem planned? _____
   _____

6. How can you guide audience expectations? _____
   _____

7. What is a capsule conclusion? A summary conclusion? _____
   _____

8. How can you effectively get your point across? _____
_____

9. Ideally, what should topic sentences achieve? _____
_____

10. What's an example of a speech vehicle you could use?_____
_____

11. If you are given a topic to speak about of which you know nothing, what
can you do? _____
_____

ANSWERS TO IMPROMPTU SPEAKING REVIEW QUESTIONS

1. Calm down.

2. Pick a purpose and pick an introduction.

3. It segues well into the body of the topic and is relatively simple.

4. Time pattern, order of importance pattern, geographical perspective, etc.

5. Use supporting materials.

6. By using verbal cues to let the audience know where you're going in your speech.

7. A capsule conclusion is when the conclusion refers back to the introduction. A summary conclusion is when you summarize your argument at the end.

8. State, demonstrate, and restate your point.

9. Topic sentences should make the argument of your speech flow logically by themselves. They serve as a road map for the audience.

10. Word or phrase motifs.

11. Use the topic as a launchpad into another topic.

IMPROMPTU SPEAKING CHECKLIST

Here are some questions to ask yourself mentally when you give an impromptu speech.

1. Have I picked a purpose for my speech?

2. What will my introduction discuss?

3. What kind of pattern of organization will I use?

4. Am I speaking in complete sentences? In paragraphs?

5. Is my argument flowing logically and am I making, demonstrating, and remaking my point?

6. Do I have any relevant supporting materials I could use?

7. What kind of conclusion do I want?

8. Could I use any kind of speech vehicle?

9. Could I use this topic as a launchpad?

10. Is the argument and the logic of my argument coming across to the audience?

Bottom line: Is the audience understanding what I am communicating to them?

CHAPTER 15

Popping the Question, and Answers

Like so many a great romance, your ultimate courting of the crowd comes when they pop the question and you give the engaging answer. Because the Q&A session following many speeches is where you seal the romantic relationship with your listeners. You always want questions because it's often your opportunity to interact with the audience. The first point to remember when preparing for questions and answers is to *anticipate the questions*. Think about them in advance. You know what the topic is; run it by people. See what questions they have for you and think about the answers you will give.

You set the agenda in most speech situations. How long do you want the question-and-answer session to be? Are you going to take questions only in writing? This can help you avoid long-winded or antagonistic questions. Are you going to allow follow-up questions? With big audiences, follow-up questions can take attention away from you as a speaker because the audience, not you, is doing the talking.

You want to ensure questions. Why do you want questions? You've finished your speech, there's applause, and then there are no questions. What does that imply? That you made no impact on the audience at all. That you bored them to tears, if not to death. That your point of view is irrelevant. You don't want that. You want it to appear as if you've got this great interactive situation. So what do you do to ensure questions?

You can always *plant questions*. Prior to your speech, a potential audience member may talk about your speech and ask a question. You can say, "That's a really good question. Would you mind asking it at the end of the program?" Later, when that person poses the question to you, it looks perfectly unrehearsed. And you're off and running.

Make it very clear you'll welcome questions. Say this: "Are there any questions? It's okay to ask. Raise your hand." If you forgot to plant a question or the plant gets shy, you don't say, "Well, I guess there are no questions, this was the most boring speech in the history of mankind. I'll sit down now." Of course, you want: two rounds of applause—you want to end with a bang, twice! So one thing you should say is "You know a question often asked of me when I deliver this presentation is . . ." *You pose the question yourself.* And you better give a good answer to your own question!

You don't want to end without any questions. So if there are two hands up in the audience, you say there's only time for one more question. That way you know you're not going to end without questions. You never let your speech languish. You need to ensure questions and keep your presentation going.

So, how do you get the second round of applause? Here's how: Prepare for your question-and-answer session even more than you prepared for your speech. What do I mean? Save stories, illustrations, quotations, interesting examples, good points, a visual aid that you didn't use in your speech, and now pull one of them out in the Q&A. The audience will think you're a genius: "What an incredible speaker, off-the-cuff he's creating visual aids."

How do you end the Q&A session? Write a *second conclusion*. When there's a second conclusion, people applaud. I'll tell you why you want a second round of applause. Have you ever been to a musical? The good ones like *Les Miserables* always end with a song, so that when you leave the theater everyone is humming the tune. They're humming your tune, because you had a great conclusion that had them applauding again.

Now that you have questions, how will you answer them? Engage the audience member first by: *listening to the question*. How many speakers start giving an answer that does not address the question? Listen, then *answer the question*. If it's a yes or no question, the first word out of your mouth, unless you're running for a political office, should be yes or no. If the question is not a yes or no question, use the syntax of the question. For example, if someone asks, "What are your feelings on the subject of——" you should respond, "My feeling on the subject of——is ..." Use the wording of the question to sound responsive.

The engaging answer is more than mere monosyllables. Answer, and then *illustrate your answer*. Use Q&A as a vehicle to continue your speech. And if you don't know the answer to the question, it's always better to acknowledge your ignorance rather than demonstrate it. Suppose you're asked a difficult and unexpected question and you don't know the answer. I always say, "That's an excellent question," and add "I don't have the precise answer, but I'd like to get back to you on that." Or perhaps I'll say, "That's an interesting question, and it raises another related topic." I keep talking so that my ignorance is not on constant display. However, what I don't do is make up an answer, because frequently the person asking the question knows the answer and will be sure to tell everyone else.

The Five Ds

Sometimes you are asked hostile questions, such as those that start off "You don't mean to tell me . . ." That's a hostile question, by tone and delivery designed to unromance the room. So what do you do when you're asked a hostile question? Use the Five Ds.

First, *delay.* Most hostile questioners want you to respond quickly, defensively, and without thinking. If you briefly delay, you're back in charge. Take a deep breath. Wait two seconds. (If you wait three seconds, the audience will think you're not going to answer or are suffering an attack of aphasia!) Then say, "Thank you for that excellent question." Calm the room and recapture the pace.

Second, *defuse* the question. That is, take out the loaded terms. When a questioner asks, "You can't possibly be in favor of killing unborn children, can you?" you reply, "The questioner is asking, What are my feelings on terminating pregnancies?" Defuse the loaded terms. They're framed that way, to make a point. The audience will not hold your reformulation against you, because they understand that the question was loaded.

Third, *dissect* the question. Most hostile questions are multiparted. Someone may keep asking you questions, and it'll be hard to know where the question mark goes. What do you do? You say, "That's an excellent question. I'd like to address both parts of it." I then write a note to myself as to the second part. I answer part one, then I look at my notes and answer part two. I write the note because most speakers don't remember the second part of a question once they finish answering the first. Then they have to say, "What was the second part of the question again?" That gives the forum back to the questioner. Remember, you're giving the speech, not him or her.

Fourth, *depersonalize* the questioner. Questioners often launch ad hominem attacks such as: "How can a fat cat lawyer like you possibly understand the concerns of poor people?" You depersonalize the question: "I believe you're asking if affluence inherently destroys compassion. I think that the acts of FDR and JFK show that this simply isn't so." You're back in charge.

Don't let the audience member become the speaker. If the questioner is going on and on, giving a mini speech, get that person to the question mark at the first breath he or she takes. You frame and complete the question. Reclaim your status as speaker: Make eye contact with the questioner, then broaden to the rest of the audience. Do not have a solo conversation with the questioner—and discourage serial, follow-up questions.

Fifth and finally, *deflect* the question if necessary. If the question is totally inappropriate, you may deflect it. If, for example, someone asks a racist question, you can say, "I'm simply not going to answer that question." When Bill Bradley was running for president, he had a simple and most engaging answer to inappropriate and invasive questions: "You may ask if I'm a criminal, but not if I'm a sinner. We're all sinners, and I'm not going to answer that question." He successfully deflected questions that sought gossip and not news.

Similarly if the question is totally off the point, then you also may deflect it. If you're giving a speech on the subject of the death penalty and someone stands up and says, "What do you think of the Giants' chances this year?" you deflect that question. But you don't say, "That's ridiculous, stop wasting our time." You're courteous and professional as you deflect the irrelevancy. There is, however, one D you should never use in response to pointed questions, the sixth D: descending to the level of the questioner. When confronted by hostile questions, don't bicker, don't fight, don't criticize, don't get mad, and don't descend to an inappropriate retort.

You stay above it all. You deflect saying, "That's a question that goes beyond the scope of my presentation today."

Bottom line: You must learn to love the Q&A. Studies show that if you really want to move your listeners, the prime time to do so is in the interactive part of the program. If you want to see a great question-and-answer session from American history, get a video of any of John F. Kennedy's press conferences. He was charming, but forceful when necessary. He seemed to love questions and answers. To be an effective communicator you need to develop the same engaging style when your audience member pops you with a question at the end of your presentation.

Q&A REVIEW QUESTIONS

1. What's the first point when preparing for a question-and-answer session?

2. What do you want to do in a question-and-answer session?

3. How can you ensure questions?

4. What are the five Ds for dealing with hostile questions?

5. What sixth D should you not use for hostile questions?

ANSWERS TO Q&A REVIEW QUESTIONS

1. Anticipate the questions.

2. Set the agenda and ensure questions.

3. Plant questions or pose them yourself.

4. Delay, defuse, dissect, depersonalize, and deflect.

5. Descend to the level of the person who posed the question.

Q&A CHECKLIST

1. What kind of agenda should I set for the Q&A?

2. What questions should I anticipate?

3. What are the questions I could pose myself?

Conclusion: Keeping the Romance Alive: Bring Flowers and Candy

Every good relationship needs excitement to fan and sometimes to rekindle the flames of romance. So, too, when romancing a room. Candy, flowers, quiet dinners at fancy restaurants, trips away for the weekend, and special anniversary plans all add spice to a relationship when the first-date jitters wear off. It's up to you as a public speaker to use the concepts we've discussed in *Romancing the Room* to add spice to your presentations long after your introductory applause has died down.

As you have read, there are many ways to keep the romance alive when speaking in public—ways to keep your audience enthralled and enthusiastic about you and your speech. Stories, visual aids, the pitch of your voice, your movement on stage, and the illustrations you use to prove your points are all examples of the "flowers and candy" that will ensure a great relationship between the speaker and the audience. Of course, this kind of embellishment may be tough at times, especially when added to the hurdle of writing a great speech. It's not enough to write a great speech—you have to give a great speech, too. Hopefully this book has given you the skills you need to deliver strong, clear, and thought-provoking speeches every time.

You don't want to go the way of the disastrous dinner date—one where the audience (like a bored dinner companion) wishes they were someplace else once you take the stage. I wish you much success in all your future public speaking engagements; stay in touch through www.wagstaffe.com. The principles you have learned in *Romancing the Room* will help you engage your audience, court your crowd, and speak successfully in public—every time.

Index